Make Every Session Count

Getting the Most Out of Your Brief Therapy

JOHN PRESTON, Psy.D.
NICOLETTE VARZOS, Ph.D.
DOUGLAS S. LIEBERT, Ph.D.

Foreword by Simon Budman, Ph.D.

New Harbinger Publications, Inc.

Publisher's Note

This publication is designed to provide accurate and authoritative information in regard to the subject matter covered. It is sold with the understanding that the publisher is not engaged in rendering psychological, financial, legal, or other professional services. If expert assistance or counseling is needed, the services of a competent professional should be sought.

Distributed in the U.S.A. by Publishers Group West; in Canada by Raincoast Books; in Great Britain by Airlift Book Company, Ltd.; in South Africa by Real Books, Ltd.; in Australia by Boobook; and in New Zealand by Tandem Press.

Copyright © 2000 by John Preston, Nicolette Varzos, and Douglas Liebert
New Harbinger Publications, Inc.
5674 Shattuck Avenue
Oakland, CA 94609

The first edition of this book was published in 1995 by Impact Publishers.

Cover design by SHELBY DESIGNS AND ILLUSTRATES
Edited by Jessica Martines
Text design by Michele Waters

Library of Congress Catalog Card Number: 99-75285
ISBN 1-57224-190-X Paperback

Printed in the United States of America

New Harbinger Publications' Website address: www.newharbinger.com

02   01   00

10   9   8   7   6   5   4   3   2   1

First printing

To Betty Preston, my mom, my friend,
and queen of the lake.
—J.P.

For my children, Tanisha and Aaron.
—N.V.

To my wife and children for what they've taught me,
and their love and support.
—D.L.

Contents

Foreword

To THE CLIENT and potential client:

Throughout health care there is an increasing emphasis on the patient/client as consumer. You are not just someone who comes in to see a therapist for treatment and passively has psychotherapy done *to* you. You have rights and responsibilities. There are ways that you can impact the course of your own therapy. I think that the best consumer is an informed consumer. I think that the best client for time-effective and brief therapy is one who is willing to fully participate as a partner in the treatment process. This book will help you in several ways. It will help you know what you are looking for from your therapy and therapist. It will also help you see how to take an active and complete role in your own improvement.

You can ask questions, change the focus of treatment, suggest certain things to your therapist about your situation that he or she may not have thought about, and so on. You can and should be a full partner in your treatment. *Every Session Counts* can help you do so.

To the therapist:

The thing I like most about this book is that it is practical. Preston, Varzos, and Liebert obviously set out to write a volume that clients and potential clients could use and that therapists could recommend. They have clearly succeeded.

I have thought about the need for a book like this many times in the past. I always look for books I can suggest to the individuals and couples I see. How to keep the therapy alive between visits is a constant question for me. How to implement Milton Erickson's sage post-hypnotic suggestion, "My voice will go with you."

If you are trying to do brief or time-effective therapy in the current health care environment, you need as many tools as possible. It is becoming increasingly important to find ways to help the people we see actively engage in the therapeutic process *outside* the confines of the office. This has always been the case, but we have had the luxury not to think too much about it. When insurance benefits covered weekly, or multiple sessions per week, if you didn't deal with an issue or the client made no progress in today's visit, maybe something would transpire in the next visit or the one after that. Few therapists can think like this anymore.

How can we, as clinicians, make every session count? In several ways: (1) *a well-prepared* client is a client who can make the most of each visit; (2) through the use of *tasks and homework* assignments that carry the session into the "real world"; (3) by being *informed* about and *skilled* in methods of brief and time-effective therapy that have demonstrated value. I think that this book will help you help your clients more effectively. It will also help them be better-informed participants in the therapy process.

—Simon H. Budman, Ph.D.
Newton, Massachusetts
July 16, 1995

Acknowledgments

PSYCHOTHERAPY WAS BORN in the early part of the twentieth century. Forms of treatment were created to help people face and survive the difficulties of life with less emotional strife. Yet until recently, most psychotherapies required a good deal of time and money. Such treatments were simply out of reach for many ordinary folks.

The names David Malan, James Mann, Gregory Bateson, Peter Sifneos, Habib Davanlo, Aaron Beck, Simon Budman, and Alan Gurman may not ring bells for those readers outside the field of psychology. But these innovative therapists have, during the past twenty-five years, pioneered approaches to emotional healing now simply referred to as "brief therapy." Their efforts have been directed toward the development of new and more effective approaches designed to reduce human emotional suffering in a much shorter period of time. We wish to acknowledge and honor these men and their work.

Many thanks to our editor, Jessica Martines, and to Michelle Riekstins for their help with the preparation of the manuscript.

Finally, heartfelt thanks to our patients, our students, and our teachers. The most important lessons we have learned regarding emotional healing have come from you.

We sincerely hope this book will be of help to you or to someone you love who is going through difficult times.

Best wishes,

John Preston, Nikki Varzos, and Doug Liebert, 2000

Thinking About Getting Some Help?

"**I**'VE HAD THIS *job for thirty years. I was at the top of my career. Then this young kid, straight out of school, with his fancy MBA comes in and pushes me out! What the hell am I supposed to do now? I've got bills to pay, kids, and now even my retirement is in question. How am I going to look in the job market now?! I feel so worthless. Nothing is right. I'm yelling at my wife for no reason and I feel terrible all the time.*"

Life really hits below the belt sometimes . . .

- Your employer just announced a 30 percent layoff.

- A loved one is killed in an accident.

- A child is diagnosed with a life-threatening illness.

- You can't keep up financially.

- A relationship is filled with anger and conflict.

- The demands of everyday living are weighing you down: picking up after the kids, cleaning the bathroom, paying bills.

Why does it seem we have to keep running harder than ever just to stay in the same place? Why is life sometimes so hard? Is it bad luck, fate, God's will, carelessness, the economy, the government, or what?

One thing we all share in common is that often life is very stressful. If you're reading this book, chances are you're looking for a way to deal more effectively with difficult times. You're used to solving your own problems, but this time you just can't seem to get a handle on it.

So you're thinking about getting some help. But the idea of therapy itself may be kind of scary. Will it help? How much will it cost? Will health insurance cover it? How do you find a therapist? Do you really want to tell a perfect stranger what's bothering you? Why can't you just solve your own problems?

In this book we'll help you answer those questions. We're going to tell you how *brief therapy* may help, what to expect if you seek therapy, and how you can help yourself improve your life.

> There are times when you may need help to deal with the distress; when life gets to be too much; when you feel you're coming apart at the seams.

As you grow older it seems that life's challenges are on the increase and staying on top of them demands enormous effort. Think about it. Is there really anyone you know who hasn't been hit with some difficult life stresses? Problems add up, they hurt, and sometimes even overwhelm us.

Guilty, sad, anxious, overburdened, depressed—have you ever felt like that? Who hasn't? Always able to cope successfully before, this time you need a little help—from more than just your friends.

Do you have to be crazy to need help? No, just human. Like this distraught parent:

"I just read my kid's diary. She's doing LSD, crank, and marijuana. I had no idea! She's just been suspended from school and wants to move out. What is she talking about? She's only fifteen years old! She stole my husband's car last night, was in a car accident, and they say it's her fault. Now what do we do?! I feel so helpless!"

Even someone who has always been able to cope well, adapt to changing situations, and survive can be overcome by a sense of helplessness and loss. It can happen to any one of us at any time. And it can make us feel guilty, powerless, victimized, and overwhelmed.

There are times when you may need help to deal with the distress: when life gets to be too much and you feel you're coming apart at the seams. You don't have to be crazy to feel like that. All you have to be is human to know that living can be hard.

Therapy? Isn't That for "Mental Illness"?

Not long ago, the idea of being "crazy" or "in therapy" brought to mind images of dark hospital corridors, locked rooms, and years of treatment from a doctor who interpreted your every word while you spilled your guts. Most of us don't have firsthand experience with psychiatric treatment, but we can readily recall motion picture or television versions. (Let's face it, graphic and sensational images sell lots of TV advertising.) As a result, lots of folks figure that if you think you need therapy you must be *really* sick.

As a culture, we've generally valued self-sufficiency, and many people have mistakenly believed that those who suffer from emotional pain are either "stupid," "bad," "weak," or "nuts." To admit that you hurt like hell can add feelings of inadequacy or shame to your pain. And, if you have the idea that therapy is only for the "seriously mentally ill," you may have kept it private and continued to suffer in silence.

The fact is that suffering is not rare and you're not alone. You hurt and are looking for something to take away the pain. Fortunately, help is available.

Lots of people go to counselors and therapists these days. From time to time everyone will feel painful disappointments, losses, and conflicts with others. What you're feeling is a common and shared human experience. And you can get help. Not the type of help that lasts twenty-five years and costs hundreds of thousands of dollars. But effective, time-limited treatment—*brief therapy*—that can help you to resolve a crisis or painful situation, often in just a few sessions.

How Can a Few Sessions Really Help?

In brief therapy *every session counts*. It's not a fad, but a form of treatment developed and refined over many years that integrates effective procedures from a number of viewpoints. And it appears on the scene just in time, since most health insurance programs now cover only limited treatment.

Brief therapy can be as effective as long-term treatment for some people and some situations. The topics we cover in this book will help you to understand a little more about brief therapy and what the choice and opportunity may mean to you.

To prepare yourself for your journey, here are a few keys to help make brief therapy work for you:

1. *Determine if brief therapy is right for you.* Learn what kind of problems respond best to brief treatment.

2. *Learn how you can make the most out of a few therapy sessions.* Become an active participant, not a "couch potato."

3. *Learn what to expect.* What brief therapy can or cannot do for you.

4. *Learn to develop effective coping skills.* Help yourself reduce stress and feel more in control of your life.

5. *Recognize that you may want treatment again.* Brief therapy focuses on your *current* problems. At different times in your life, as new challenges appear, you can choose to come back if you need help in the future.

Remember, it's your life. You hold the key and the choice is yours. By seeking therapy, you are choosing to take responsibility for your life; to recognize and acknowledge your pain and humanness, and to find new strength within yourself. To help with this process, we'll be exploring what you can do to better problem-solve and cope in Part III of this book, "A Coping Skills Manual." We'll also explore the role of medications and let you know how to use your community mental health service, university counseling center, or managed health care plan most effectively and efficiently.

Let's get started.

PART I

What Is Brief Therapy?

Chapter 1

Is Brief Better?

WHEN YOU'RE REALLY sick, you probably make an appointment with your physician. The physician examines you, prescribes medicine, and—with time and good fortune—you're well again.

Psychotherapy began with a similar model: the "powerful doctor" healed the "sick patient." The patient may not have chosen to see a therapist, but was too ill to resist. It was generally assumed that a mentally ill patient would need treatment for a long time, if not forever. The relationship between the therapist and the patient reflected an unequal division of power, with the patient holding the short straw. Those earlier patients saw a therapist because they were "sick," not because of the problems of daily living.

Today people often make the choice to see a professional therapist—counselor, clinical social worker, marriage and family therapist, pastoral counselor, psychologist, or psychiatrist—when life feels too hard to deal with alone.

Today's clients know they won't be in therapy for twenty years or have to recount every detail of childhood. This is not to say that long-term therapy doesn't have its place. Brief therapy is not for everyone, nor is it appropriate for every problem (more on this in chapter 7). But for many people, a brief intervention can offer much needed help, support, and emotional relief.

Hire a Consultant!

If your finances are complex, or if you're having financial problems, you might decide to hire an accountant. The accountant would assist you in creative problem solving, show you how to work out your difficulties with income, expenses, and taxes. And ultimately help you to make the best choices.

Similarly, if you were physically out of shape and decided to get healthy, you might go to a gym and hire a fitness instructor. A fitness professional would assess your condition, guide you through exercises appropriate to your current abilities and physical state, and help you choose exercises suited to your particular needs and goals.

When living gets hard, you could go shopping (some folks call this "retail therapy"). You may find temporary relief—or escape—this way. However, short-term solutions are often not the answer. It is likely that you'll get more in the long run if you hire a mental health consultant.

Is your mental health as important to you as your physical well-being? You don't stay in shape by being lucky, you have to work at it. A strong marriage is the result of hard work. And a healthy mind and attitude may at times require a little outside help and maintenance—a "tune-up" for how you think and feel.

When you view a therapist as your mental health consultant, the unequal division of power seen in earlier years is gone. You alone made the decision to enter therapy—no one made that decision for you. You may be in pain and seeking relief, but that doesn't mean that you can't be an educated and informed consumer.

> The best, most effective way to feel better is to become an active and knowledgeable participant in your treatment process.

Your mental health consultant is there for you as a facilitator of change, healing, and growth. Like the fitness consultant who doesn't "cure" but provides direction, guidance, and support, the mental health consultant is an agent of change working with you, to help you through difficult times. A therapist can, for example, help you to learn more effective problem-solving skills, resulting in greater self-confidence and increased ability to cope with your current problems.

Maybe you'd prefer to be your own mental health consultant? Here are a couple of things to keep in mind: emotional pain is considerably more intense when it is experienced alone and none of us can be completely objective about our own circumstances.

Your mental health consultant won't and can't do the work for you, but will listen objectively and help guide you toward the results that *you* choose. Each life experience gives you and your consultant the chance to examine your thoughts, beliefs, perceptions, and attitudes and how they work for and against you in your daily living.

Your therapist isn't there to "fix" or "change" you, but to build on your strengths. A consultant is your guide to understanding the complex nature of stressful events and how they are related to your thoughts, attitudes, and beliefs about yourself and your world.

A therapist/consultant can help you reduce your pain, minimize future disasters, and develop action plans and strategies for growth and healing, now and in the future. The emphasis in brief therapy is not on "sick patients" and "powerful doctors." It's on people in distress making wise choices so they can take charge of their lives.

Why Brief Therapy?

Since psychotherapy arrived on the scene in the early part of the twentieth century, this form of treatment has been considered a lengthy endeavor. Therapists advocating traditional Freudian analysis insisted for therapy to be beneficial, it had to be intense and long-term. Those few who were able to afford it entered analysis and visited their therapist three to five times a week for many months, and often many years. Psychoanalysis was often helpful for this small group of clients, and, because it was the treatment of choice for the "rich and famous," it became the approach glorified by the media and desired by the rest of the population.

What's wrong with this picture? First, long-term psychotherapy is extremely expensive and therefore out of reach for most people. Human emotional suffering is widespread and affects people from all walks of life, rich and poor alike. Second, extensive research finds little compelling scientific evidence that, overall, long-term psychotherapy is more effective than brief therapy. In fact, the majority of people looking for therapy prefer short-term psychotherapy and greatly benefit from the experience.

What Is "Brief Therapy"?

Generally brief therapy is defined as psychotherapy lasting from one to twenty sessions. In the contemporary "managed care" environment, and in most public treatment settings (community mental health, university counseling centers), brief therapy averages between three and twelve sessions.

This shorter course of treatment—fewer sessions and significantly lower costs—makes psychotherapy available to more people.

In the United States more than 8 million people see a therapist each year and 85% of them are treated with brief therapy.

Sometimes therapy must be brief because insurance companies, mental health clinics, counseling centers, and HMOs have limits on the mental health benefits that they offer. However, short-term psychotherapy is often brief by design. Short-term therapy includes special techniques that can speed up the process, and the results are often better than for long-term therapy.

Brief therapy, however, is defined not only by the length of treatment. There are a number of goals and characteristics of brief therapy that set it apart from longer forms of psychological treatment. The key elements include:

- Focus on a *specific problem*, not on "reshaping your personality"
- *Active involvement* of both client and therapist
- Emphasis on *solutions*, not causes to life problems
- *Time-limited* course of treatment

  We'll take a look at how it works in the next chapter.

Chapter 2

Off the Couch and into Action

Most brief therapy approaches are "action oriented." Every session really does count. With only a few sessions available clients cannot afford to be passive or to gradually explore their concerns, feelings, and past and present experiences. The process requires rapid identification of and attention to the primary area of greatest current concern. Therapists call this establishing a *focus*.

It's not that other issues or life experiences are unimportant. In brief therapy, you and your therapist together will identify and agree to work on *the* most important or urgent concerns in your life right now (this may be, for a particular symptom, such as depression or panic attacks, a particular life struggle, such as resolving conflicts with an employer, or learning more effective ways to resolve marital problems). Once you and your therapist have clearly identified "the problem," this focus becomes the central issue to be discussed in therapy sessions.

- A second way brief therapy is "active" is that the therapist is more likely to speak out in therapy sessions. In some forms of therapy the therapist stays pretty quiet; in brief therapy there generally are more questions, answers, feedback and active problem solving.

- A third way brief therapy is lively is that it really encourages the client to *take action*. This may be in the form of between-session homework assignments (keeping a personal journal, monitoring progress using self-rating checklists, trying out new behaviors in life situations). A lot goes on outside the therapy room and between sessions. Many clients enjoy these activities that make them active participants in their treatment, feeling that they are better able to "take charge."

- Another way that brief therapy is action oriented is through developing the client's "tool kit" for dealing with stressful situations, including life skills for:
  - *Interpersonal coping*—more effective and practical ways to problem-solve and resolve conflicts with friends, relatives, co-workers, and important others
  - *Internal stress reduction*—powerful ways to reduce anxiety, sadness, despair, and irritability.

One important benefit of increasing your coping skills is that you may discover these skills offer you a greater sense of control and mastery in everyday life situations, reducing feelings of helplessness and powerlessness. Coping skills may be taught in individual or group therapy sessions, or with the use of self-help books. Part III of this book provides a brief coping skills manual describing a number of effective approaches. You may find this helpful as you are going through your brief therapy experience.

No one ever gets completely "cured," 100 percent emotionally healthy or immune to the pain of human experiences of loss, disappointment, or frustration.

Living life, meeting challenges, surviving hard times, and growing are lifelong processes. Brief therapy can best be seen as an important experience or tool that helps people as they hit those inevitable hard times throughout life. The goal of brief therapy is not to cure, but to provide support, facilitate growth, and increase effective coping.

Research shows that people can change and experience benefits while *in* brief therapy, but it doesn't end there. A good deal of growth and "work" continues after therapy has ended. The last session of brief therapy, in a very real sense, is not *the end*. After the final session, clients put newly learned skills into action, acting as their own "therapist." Following a course of brief therapy, one of the authors received a note from a woman client stating:

"I stopped coming to therapy sessions three months ago, but it's like I'm still in treatment. I often hear your voice in my mind saying, 'Remember to be decent to yourself' or 'It's okay to give yourself permission to be who you are and to feel what you feel.' . . . I also kinda do therapy with myself . . . and it helps a lot."

The time spent in therapy may be "brief," but life doesn't stop handing us challenges, frustrations, joys, and hopes. No one ever stops growing; no one ever has it all figured out.

It is not uncommon for clients to go through two or more courses of brief therapy, at various times in life. At twenty-four, Sara saw a therapist seven times for help as her marriage floundered and she and her husband became more distant with each other. She also attended a group for couples. The therapy and support group helped Sara and Ken find new ways of balancing their relationship, and they stayed together. Nine years later, following the death of her mother, Sara returned to her therapist to help her deal with her loss. They met for six sessions, though her grieving continued well past the time of her last session. However, therapy helped her to accept the reality of her mom's death and the depth of her sorrow. She began to feel more "okay" about expressing her sadness to her husband and her kids. She was clearly on the road to emotional healing from this painful life event.

Therapy is not a magical solution or a cure-all for the painful things that happen to us as human beings. Brief therapy can, however, be a tremendously important resource during painful times, and a foundation for successfully handling the tough times that may come later.

Chapter 3

What's Therapy Like?

IT'S NOT WHAT you think.

You've had glimpses of psychotherapy in books, in the movies, and on television. Forget that. It's not likely that what you've seen has prepared you for what really goes on.

If you're like most folks, you're thinking about therapy because you're experiencing significant distress or emotional pain—perhaps desperation—in your life. (Almost no one goes to therapy for the small stuff.) Under such times of great stress and personal uncertainty, everyone wants and needs to feel safe, and to feel some assurance that the decision to see a therapist was the right one.

Most people have lots of questions about this business of telling their troubles to a total stranger:

"What actually happens in therapy?"

"What can I expect to get from therapy?"

"What are realistic and attainable benefits I might gain from therapy?"

"Is there a reasonable chance of getting the help I need?"

"Will it be worth the time, money, effort, and emotional investment to become involved in a course of brief therapy?"

Good questions! In the following chapters we are going to offer you some straight talk about psychotherapy, and present how some people benefit from their experience of brief therapy. As we address your expectations, we'll focus on three topics: what's expected of you, what actually happens during therapy sessions, and in the next chapter, what therapists are really like.

What's Expected of You

You may be asked to fill out a background questionnaire to help the therapist determine if treatment with you is appropriate, and as a means of learning details of your history (educational history, number of people in your family, prior psychotherapy experiences, medical history . . .).

- You will be asked to do your best at sharing openly your particular concerns, thoughts, and feelings.

- You may be asked to complete assigned and agreed tasks—homework assignments—outside the therapy hour. (More about this in chapter 16.)

- You will be expected to show up for sessions as scheduled and to pay agreed-upon professional fees. And to give advance notice in case of a cancellation (except in cases of last-minute emergencies).

- You may be asked to complete one or more psychological tests to help your therapist assess your personal situation and needs.

What Actually Happens during Therapy Sessions?

Therapy sessions vary, depending on who you are, what current problems you're experiencing, and the kind of therapist you hire. We can, however, give you a summary glimpse of the "typical" course of brief therapy.

PHASE ONE: Getting Acquainted and Discussing What Concerns You Most. Effective therapists often help the therapy process get under way by asking their clients, "What are the main reasons you've decided to come to therapy?" or "I'd like to know what's most on your mind and what you'd like to accomplish in coming to therapy." The early sessions generally are designed to help you feel more at ease and begin discussing your main problems or concerns. At this beginning phase, many people entering therapy are unclear about what they are feeling, or they may be self-critical, for example, "I shouldn't be feeling this way." You and your therapist will be forming a "therapeutic alliance"—a working partnership that will help you get past your uncertainty and reach your goals in therapy.

PHASE TWO: Finding a Focus. As the discussion continues in further sessions, your therapist will do a lot of listening and ask questions to help you pinpoint a major focus—the major issue or problem you'll be dealing with in therapy. You and your therapist will identify specific problems, and find out in what ways these issues are especially important to you at this time in your life.

Psychotherapy (brief or long-term) doesn't provide a quick fix. In fact, people may find that they feel somewhat worse during the first couple of sessions—at least more keenly aware of distressing feelings. And the reality often is that once a person begins to take a close look at difficult issues, emotional pain may be felt more intensely. If this happens to you, *don't bail out!* It's natural, normal, and fairly predictable—but an essential part of coming to terms with life issues that hurt. Fortunately for most, emotional distress at some point subsides as they begin to get a handle on life problems and cope more effectively.

PHASE THREE: Refocusing or Tuning into the Problem. A common experience during the third phase of brief therapy is for clients to begin to understand their problems, and themselves, in a new light. Many times this involves a change of perspective and attitude. Such "problems" as being oversensitive to criticism, feeling taken advantage of by others, missing a loved one who has died, feeling overwhelmed and frustrated at work, start to seem more "understandable." The problems may seem just as painful, undesirable, or frustrating; however, many folks start to think, "My feelings make sense to me now" or "Of course I feel this way." The volume gets turned down on harsh self-criticism.

Attitudes Can Shift during Therapy

From	To
This is crazy.	I don't like the way this feels.
I shouldn't be so upset.	I'm upset. What can I do about it?
This shouldn't be happening!	I don't want this to happen, but it is and it's upsetting.
I'm confused. What the hell is the matter with me?	Of course I feel this way!

PHASE FOUR: Action-Oriented Skills . . . Practice, Practice, Practice. "I am more aware of what I feel and I don't condemn myself so harshly. But I still feel bad. What do I do next?"

Often in brief therapy, once the major problems or concerns have been clarified, the focus is shifted toward active problem solving. Kimberly, for example, learned ways to reduce anxiety by providing inner support for herself prior to taking an exam at school. Roberto developed assertive ways to communicate his feelings and needs to his wife. In one of his therapy sessions, Doug carefully planned out just how he was going to approach his shop foreman to share concerns he had about his work environment. Sherri began to write in her personal journal, discovered more about her own feelings, and learned to give herself permission to grieve the loss of her brother.

Brief therapy became a place for these people to think things through, come to conclusions regarding actions they wanted to take, learn some new coping skills, and practice these skills during the session. As Roberto said, "Having a therapist is kinda like having a coach. You can plan out what you want to do, practice it, get some feedback, refine it, and then get the extra push you need to do it for real in your life."

PHASE FIVE: Fine Tuning. In the final stages of brief therapy, it is often helpful to summarize what's happened. It helps to be clear about several points:

- This was my problem

- I came to see it as understandable ... not "crazy"

- I felt okay about wanting to make a change

- I figured out which approaches work for me and which don't

- I felt supported by my therapist

- I put coping skills into action

- I got some results

Getting better and feeling better usually aren't just due to fate or good luck. You have to work at changing and discovering what helps.

Once you know how to cope more successfully you're better prepared for the next time life becomes difficult.

Of course, it's not all this simple! Experiences vary. But the phases we've talked about here describe a common experience in brief therapy. Most people who succeed in therapy typically don't feel ultimately "cured" or "fixed," but they do feel better. They leave therapy knowing that they've done some *real work*, and it was *their effort* that paid off. In particular, the most common outcome of successful brief therapy is feeling okay about who you are!

Some of the specific results you may realistically expect from brief therapy are discussed in Chapter 7. But first, let's take a look at this person we call "therapist."

Chapter 4

What Are Therapists Like?

THERAPISTS ARE human beings.

"Obviously," you may say. But some folks seem to think that therapy is an art, practiced by individuals with X-ray vision and wise advice for every problem. The fact is that therapists are highly trained experts in human behavior who are just as vulnerable as the rest of the population to all of the realities of being human.

In this chapter, we'll review the characteristics that allow a professional therapist to offer that special "helping relationship" that assists people in making sense of their lives during stressful times.

What Makes Therapists Different?

- *Therapists generally don't give advice.* Many people can benefit from helpful suggestions and good advice from time to time, but such input is readily available from friends and relatives (even when you don't want it). Truth be told, most therapists aren't really any better at giving commonsense advice than anyone else. But they can and do provide a kind of help not readily found in your ordinary network of family and friends.

- *Therapists are trained to understand emotional distress and the process of emotional healing.* In a sense they are people who understand the general terrain of the human landscape, and can help guide people through painful times toward growth and healing.

- *Therapists are willing and able to face very strong emotions.* It's hard to really be with someone when they are experiencing intense feelings. To witness a human suffering in itself is difficult. It is also hard for many people to experience another's pain without it touching on their own inner feelings. Good therapists have learned to handle these issues: to be fully present with their clients, resonate with their pain, but also maintain an appropriate objectivity. A client is able to express strong feelings and knows that the therapist cares, yet is not overwhelmed or blown away by the powerful emotions. This provides a considerable amount of stability and safety within the therapy hour.

> Good therapists have learned to be fully present with their patients . . . to transmit an attitude of respect, understanding, and acceptance.

- *Good therapists tend to be nonjudgmental.* They understand that most interpersonal and emotional problems can be seen as attempts to emotionally survive the common problems in living. Effective therapists transmit an attitude of respect, understanding, and acceptance. In psychotherapy outcome studies, the most commonly reported factor judged to have been helpful to clients was the therapist's ability to genuinely care and to understand the client. The therapist's compassionate attitude helps the client to reduce excessive self-criticism and develop an enhanced capacity for self-acceptance.

- *Therapists provide support for self-expression.* Support and encouragement of honest expression helps shore up and solidify the development of the self. To use an analogy, when building a concrete wall, boards are used to provide support for the concrete as it begins to harden. At some point the boards can be removed and the wall is solid; the concrete has developed its own strength and it can stand on its own. In therapy, it begins to feel okay to talk openly about how things really are. Although reduction of emotional distress (decreased depression, anxiety, tension, etc.) is a primary goal for most people entering treatment, one of the most common results of psychotherapy is an increased sense of self and self-esteem. "When my therapist really listens, I know it's okay to be me!"

- *Therapists help clients to maintain a sense of realistic hope during difficult times.* Not the phony "Everything will be all right" hope, but a realistic perspective and trust in the process that psychotherapy will very likely lead to healing or better coping skills.

- *Therapists do not repeat maladaptive patterns of interaction.* Many relationships involve patterns. A dependent, seemingly helpless person may frequently enter into relationships where her behavior leads others to treat her like a child. This repetitive "interpersonal dance" may feel good at first (because it is familiar), but ultimately contributes to keeping her stuck; she never grows up. The tendency for others to rush in and rescue this "helpless" person keeps her stuck in an infantile position. A good therapist would empathize with her distress, but would resist the urge to treat her like a helpless child. The therapist's refusal to perpetuate the dance allows this client to grow and come to feel her own strength.

What You Can Expect from the Therapist

All competent psychotherapists are committed to a code of ethics and a standard of practice that attempts to assure the following (essential ingredients in a helping relationship):

- Provide privacy and confidentiality.*

- Treat clients in a decent and respectful manner.

- Gain the client's informed consent for any procedures undertaken in the course of therapy.

- Provide realistic emotional support.

- Help you feel at ease during the first meetings. Many people are worried about the first session: "I won't know what to say or where to start," "I feel anxious about talking to someone I don't know." These concerns are common and understandable; it's normal to feel nervous during the first session. Effective therapists know how to help people get started talking.

- Provide a "neutral," noncritical, and nonjudgmental environment. An important goal in therapy is not to judge people, but to understand and be helpful.

- To be honest. Your therapist is there to help you fully understand yourself, your patterns of behavior, and your feelings. The therapist's function is to provide honest and objective feedback about your attitudes and actions. The feedback will feel good when it recognizes your strengths and it may feel uncomfortable when it points out your weaknesses. Brief therapy can help you capitalize on your strengths and transform your weaknesses. The process may be uncomfortable at times, but the outcome may be positive, even more than you expect.

- Maintain a professional relationship. This is what psychotherapists refer to as "maintaining appropriate professional boundaries." It is a part of the therapists' ethical codes to assure that therapy remains safe. In the practice of psychotherapy, relating to a patient in other-than-professional ways—socially, romantically, or entering

---

* In most states laws regarding confidentiality are limited; i.e., there are certain instances when confidentiality does not apply. See Appendix A for specifics on confidentiality.

into a business relationship—is inappropriate, and may be unethical or illegal. Sexually intimate relationships are absolutely prohibited by the professional codes of ethics (and the law in most states). Social friendships outside the therapy hour and business deals are unwise, and may also be unethical.

- Make appropriate referrals. Sometimes your therapist may need to refer you to a medical doctor, for a psychiatric evaluation and possible medication treatment. They may refer you to another therapist who offers particular services, (marital counseling), or support groups or programs when appropriate (Alcoholics Anonymous, bereavement support groups, etc.). Your therapist may even refer you to another therapist if both of you feel that the current therapy isn't working.

- Provide information about the therapist's education and training, fees, type of services offered, and responses to any number of relevant questions regarding the treatment they provide.

Types of Mental Health Therapists

Psychiatrists (M.D.): Psychiatrists are medical doctors who have received specialized training in the treatment of emotional problems, including both medication and psychological treatments. (It is possible for a physician to practice psychiatry without specialized training; however, very few do so.) Most psychiatrists treat emotional disorders with medications. Some psychiatrists also provide psychotherapy, behavior therapy, or cognitive therapy.

Psychologists: Almost all hold a doctorate degree in psychology (Ph.D., Psy.D., Ed.D.), have a number of years of postgraduate training in psychological methods, and in most states are licensed or certified to practice. They also have specialized training in the administration and interpretation of psychological tests.

Clinical Social Workers: Generally hold a master's degree (M.S.W.), have considerable supervised experience and are usually licensed by the state ("L.C.S.W."—Licensed Clinical Social Worker).

Marriage Family and Child Counselors/Therapists: A number of states grant a license or certificate to marriage, family and child counselors (or marriage, family and child therapists). Such therapists generally have at least a master's degree in counseling (M.S. or M.A.), usually with specialization in treatment of marriage and family problems and the treatment of children and adolescents.

Pastoral Counselors: Some clergy have received training in counseling and may provide supportive therapy to members of their church or to others desiring a therapist who addresses both emotional and spiritual concerns.

Getting the Most from Your Therapist

- *The chemistry has to be "good enough."* You need to feel a degree of comfort and compatibility with your therapist. Not all people are going to make a good connection. It may not be essential to feel 100 percent comfortable with your therapist, but it is quite important to feel the following: a basic sense of trust, the perception that you and your feelings are being treated with respect, and some degree of confidence that your therapist is competent. First and foremost competent therapists, beyond being well-trained and skilled, need to be good, decent people.

- *The type of treatment must be appropriate.* Not all problems are best approached in the same manner. A good therapist will evaluate your situation and within the first session or two talk with you about what kind of treatment they recommend. Some types of emotional problems are due, either in part or in full, to medical/biochemical disturbances. Medical treatment and/or psychiatric medication treatment may be helpful or even necessary (see chapter 18).

- *The treatment must do no harm.* Any approach that is powerful enough to help can be powerful enough to cause harm, if in the hands of an incompetent or destructive therapist. Most licensed therapists are well trained and are helpful to most of their clients. However, as in any other profession, incompetence and/or unethical behavior does exist. *You are entitled to competent and ethical treatment.* Anything else should be reported to appropriate institutional or regulatory agencies.

Chapter 5

Realistic Results

"FROM MISERABLE to marvelous!"

So boasted a recent ad for a psychotherapist in the Yellow Pages. Such promises of miraculous "transformation," in our opinion, are at best misguided, and at worst unethical, preying on the desperate needs of suffering and vulnerable people.

At the heart of psychotherapy is a commitment to the truth. Well-trained therapists know the benefits of psychological treatment and the limitations. In all honesty, there is no way to ever know for sure ahead of time how much you may benefit from treatment. All that is really known is that effective treatments do exist and large-scale outcome studies have shown that the majority of clients can benefit from brief therapy. The fact also remains that some people do not benefit—and some (a small minority) get worse.

Many times psychotherapy is literally "life saving" (for example, in helping to prevent suicide). However, for most people, brief therapy is likely to yield less dramatic positive benefits. As we examine some common outcomes from brief therapy in this chapter, remember that there is no guarantee that everyone will benefit. Nevertheless, these do represent realistic and rather typical results.

- *Feeling less depressed, anxious, and tense.**

---

* Psychotherapy outcome research has shown that symptom reduction (specifically anxiety and depression) is one of the most significant and common results from brief therapy. Often short-term treatment for anxiety and depression may involve both psychotherapy and psychiatric medicine (see Chapter 18).

- *Feeling better about who you are and your ability to manage your life.* This can take many forms. Before beginning therapy, many people erroneously conclude, "I'm crazy ... I'm neurotic ... I'm weak and inadequate" ... or, "I'm screwed up." For many, many psychotherapy clients, an important experience in therapy is developing a new view or belief about themselves. Negative, self-critical views, like those noted above, usually give way to compassionate, more realistic beliefs: "Of course I'm sad ... this is what people feel when they've had a serious loss" ... or, "I *am* sensitive to criticism and it irritates me when my wife is overly critical toward me" ... or, "I certainly don't like feeling so upset by this rejection, but I understand why it hurts so much. This relationship meant a lot to me!"

  The acceptance of such views can lead to changes in how you feel about yourself. Therapy clients commonly adopt healthier attitudes toward themselves.

- *"Getting clear."* Clients typically experience increased clarity about how they really feel about things, what they want and need, what they value, how they see other people, and what things in life really matter to them.

Among the myriad inner feelings, beliefs, and thoughts you hold, many were taught to you by your parents, teachers, and other influential people during your early years. Such "implanted" beliefs and thoughts (what some psychologists call "injunctions") may be helpful and agree with your own personal values: "I really am a good-hearted person" or "It's important to try my best at tasks that are challenging."

Unfortunately, implanted thoughts can also be self-critical or negative: "You're just going to fail no matter what you do, so why try?" or "Real men don't cry, so if I cry, I should feel ashamed."

Have you heard—or told yourself—any of these?

As you begin to talk openly and honestly about your thoughts and feelings, a common outcome is that you will, at some point, become clearer about which thoughts and beliefs arise from your inner, true self, and which feel somewhat alien.

Common Negative Injunctions

Don't be emotional.	Don't cry.
Don't rock the boat.	Don't get your hopes up.
Grow up! Don't be childish.	Don't ask for strokes.
Don't get too close.	Don't really trust people.
Don't trust your feelings, body, gut reactions.	Don't do better than mom/dad.
Don't get mad.	Be logical.
Be perfect.	Be strong.
Please others.	Try harder, stick with it, don't give up, don't let go.

Becoming clear about how you really feel (beliefs, thoughts, values) can be important in two respects. First, you are in a better position to make decisions or take actions that "feel right" based on your true inner beliefs. This may lead to greater ease in decision making and an increased sense of self-confidence. Second, a common result is a better developed *sense of self.* This last experience is a bit hard to define, but is an important and common outcome. It is often described by people as feeling more "real," "alive," "authentic," or "whole," and feeling better able to hold on to the inner awareness of "what I truly want, desire, believe in, or need" (see chapter 17).

As you begin to talk openly and honestly about your thoughts and feelings, you will become clearer about which thoughts and beliefs arise from your inner, true self, and which feel somewhat alien.

- *Accepting yourself.* Stressful life events often make us feel anger or fear. Yet, for many of us, to actually admit these feelings to ourselves or to express such emotions leads to feelings of shame, self-criticism, or anxiety. A common outcome from brief therapy is a new sense of okay-ness about being "you," accepting who you are, and expressing it without shame or self-criticism.

- *Developing effective problem-solving skills, ways of coping with stress, and new approaches to handling interpersonal problems.*

- *Learning important life lessons* (Strupp 1969):
  - I may have some shortcomings, but I am what I am, and that's not so bad.
  - Some emotional pain is inevitable and, in the long run, probably necessary. You can't just grit your teeth and hope it will go away. Losses have to be mourned.
  - In most instances, the expression of feelings is not dangerous (expressing anger or sadness).
  - I have a right to be who I am ... to be true to myself (values, beliefs, lifestyle), even though some people may not agree or be able to accept me.
  - Life may seem unbearable during a tremendously painful situation, but you ultimately survive.
  - It's easy to lose perspective when you are in the middle of stressful times; yet most of the time, even very difficult circumstances only last a while. With time, most people discover inner strengths and resources, and are able to get back on their feet and move ahead with their lives.
  - Sometimes you have to modify your wishes and hopes, learn to endure frustration and accept "half a loaf."
  - Wishing doesn't produce results. In order to reach goals, one needs to act, to take specific action steps.
  - You can't always get what you want.
  - Certain ways of thinking, acting and behaving, interpersonal behaviors and attitudes simply don't work and in the long run are self-defeating. In general,

"cooperation" is a good technique for getting along with people.

- If you take a good, honest look at your early life—the way you were treated, the general emotional atmosphere in your home—it will probably begin to make sense to you why certain things are especially emotionally painful (for example, in a family atmosphere of extreme shaming and criticism, it is understandable that a person might grow up being especially sensitive to criticism).
- Ultimately you are responsible for your own actions.
- Honesty (generally) is the best policy.

You may never come to agree with all of these ideas, but we encourage you to work toward a positive view of the capacity to *direct your own life*. This, after all, may be the single most important lesson of all.

Chapter 6

When Brief Is Not Enough

EVEN THOUGH BRIEF therapy can be very helpful for many people, it is not always the appropriate course of action.

Sometimes, brief psychotherapy is simply not enough. Some people have gone through tremendously difficult times and have deep emotional wounds that require longer treatment. Their problems involve not just one major focus, but several. Serious difficulties may affect many aspects of life. Brief therapy can provide a starting point for such folks, and many are able to make some gains. But those who have a lot of healing or growth to do, while able to benefit from brief treatment, may subsequently enter either a support group or longer-term therapy.

For two types of emotional problems, brief therapy is probably not a good idea at all. Those who have experienced *extreme* psychological traumas in childhood (physical, emotional, or sexual abuse or severe neglect) find that the intensity and depth of their emotional pain may not be adequately addressed in brief therapy. For them, there is the risk that a little therapy may open up emotional floodgates, without the opportunity to truly resolve and work through the pain. In such cases, brief therapy can be worse than ineffective—it can be harmful.

People with severe, chronic mental illnesses (schizophrenia, manic-depressive or bipolar illness, severe personality disorders) are not likely to benefit much from brief therapy. These major emotional disorders almost always require long-term supportive treatment and/or psychiatric medication.

Some symptoms always warrant a referral for intensive psychiatric treatment. Here's a brief summary of signs of serious psychiatric illness:

- Extreme confusion, erratic behavior, hallucinations, and abnormally unrealistic thoughts are signs of *psychosis* (for example, schizophrenia).

- Severe mood swings and manic episodes (times of very high energy, agitation, decreased need for sleep, rapid speech) may indicate *bipolar (manic-depressive) disorder.*

- A history of intense, often chaotic relationships with others; intense, volatile emotions of jealousy, anger, hostility, loneliness; bouts of severe drug or alcohol abuse, multiple suicide attempts, and/or self-mutilation all may be signs of *severe personality disorders.*

- Severe eating disorders such as anorexia nervosa (extreme weight loss, preoccupation with weight, a distorted perception of body image). This is a severe and sometimes life threatening psychiatric disorder and is not amenable to brief therapy.

- Significant alcohol or other substance abuse. Brief therapy may be helpful, but only after one has successfully attained sobriety. Such individuals *must* first seek treatment from a twelve-step program such as Alcoholics Anonymous or a professional chemical dependency treatment program.

. . . Major emotional disorders almost always require long-term supportive treatment and/or psychiatric medication.

The bottom line: The conditions summarized above indicate a number of exceptions, but the vast majority of people seeking psychotherapy can and do benefit from brief approaches. Chances are you'll find it valuable if your own circumstances do not involve one of these more serious conditions.

Long-Term Psychotherapy: Another Formula for Healing and Growth

Some emotional difficulties clearly require intensive and lengthy psychological treatment. However, you don't need to be in serious emotional pain to benefit from long-term therapy. As we've seen, brief therapy can help most people deal with fairly specific life problems, but many folks have chosen longer-term treatment for resolution of psychological issues and personal growth. As we sing the praises of brief therapy, we certainly don't want to overlook or underrate the value of long-term psychotherapeutic treatment.

PART II

How Does
Therapy Help?

Y OU'LL BENEFIT MORE from therapy if you understand how the process works. Not all approaches to psychotherapy are alike. Although most forms of therapy share some common characteristics (the provision of a safe, respectful, and confidential relationship), specific approaches and techniques have been developed that have been shown to be especially effective in dealing with particular psychological problems. In the following chapters we will outline and describe various approaches to therapy. We want to give you a glimpse of what actually happens in therapy and how it can help people to cope more effectively, to heal from emotional wounds or trauma, and/or to experience enhanced personal growth. We will also share with you information (from research studies) that indicate which approaches are best suited for which particular psychological problems or disorders. We feel strongly that everyone considering psychotherapy should be well informed so that they will know (more or less) what to expect and so that they will be able to seek out the most appropriate type of therapy.

A host of common emotional and psychological problems can be addressed by what is generally referred to as "talk therapy." Such problems include, but are not limited to the following:

- Dealing with significant, recent life stresses
- Bereavement which has become either prolonged and/or is resulting in intense or overwhelming emotional pain
- Adjusting to and coping with new life circumstances (for example, aging, retirement, taking a new job, significant medical illnesses or disability, etc.)
- Long-standing personality problems, including:
  - inadequately developed sense of identity/self
  - passivity, nonassertiveness, timidity
  - excessive emotional sensitivity, tendency to take things personally or to overreact
  - difficulties with intimacy and/or commitment
  - indecisiveness, procrastination, self-doubt
  - lack of motivation or excessive feelings of inhibition
  - chronic feelings of bitterness, pessimism, or negativity
  - long-standing, unresolved conflicts with others (resentment, anger, disappointment)
  - psychosomatic symptoms (for example, tension head-aches, fatigue, and insomnia)
  - chronic worry
  - loneliness
  - shyness
  - feelings of inadequacy
  - communication problems
- Interpersonal problems (for example, parent-child con-flicts, marital problems)
- Facing difficult circumstances for which one needs thoughtful consideration and/or support
- "Unfinished business" (old, unresolved wounds from an earlier time in one's life)

In chapters 8-12 we will describe common and basic elements of "talk therapy." These chapters will introduce you to five key themes that are felt to be essential ingredients in therapy.

Beginning in chapter 13, we will discuss and describe specific approaches that have a proven track record of effectiveness in treating the following psychological disorders: depression, panic disorder, social anxiety (also referred to as social phobia), post-traumatic stress disorder (PTSD), obsessive-compulsive disorder (OCD), and generalized anxiety (persistent, chronic anxiety).

Chapter 7

From Distress
to Healing

STRESS IS A PART of everyone's life.

We all encounter ordinary daily stresses and, sooner or later, everyone will experience especially difficult (sometimes tragic) events. Some degree of emotional suffering is unavoidable. This is just the truth . . . part of the price of membership in the human race.

Job stress, marital conflicts, on-going medical problems or chronic pain, financial worries, fears about the future, betrayal by a good friend, the list goes on. As we go through difficult times, we all have inner reactions. Whether or not our emotions are expressed outwardly has a lot to do with our culture and society, our upbringing (some people are raised to stifle emotions, grit their teeth, and be "tough"), and personality style (some folks are simply private people, who prefer to deal with emotions in an internal way).

However, *major stressful events nearly always have an impact on people*. It is rare to simply feel no effect of major distressing events. If the event is devastating enough, some individuals will bury their emotional responses. Nevertheless, those responses almost always find an outlet—somehow, at some point in time.

To successfully make it through hard times and to benefit from therapy, you must to a degree face the reality of your pain (sadness, frustration, anger, fear, loneliness . . .). At the same time, let's be clear: *There is nothing inherently noble about suffering great pain.* Some people say that it builds character or is some kind of spiritual test of strength. But the bottom line is that pain hurts, and it is very normal to want to reduce suffering.

Dealing with Emotional Pain: Mind . . . Body . . . Action!

There are three main paths we follow as we try to deal with emotional pain. Whether a conscious choice or an "automatic response," the key avenues are the mind, the body, and direct action:

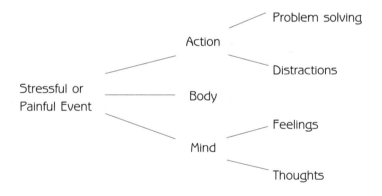

Action

Overt action generally has two aims: problem solving or distraction. Problem solving may involve going directly to a person with whom there is a conflict, speaking with him or her, and asking for some kind of change in behavior or other resolution. Distracting actions, on the other hand, are usually taken to help ignore or minimize emotional pain or distress. Examples of such actions include: workaholism, watching TV, engaging in sports, numbing oneself with alcohol, tranquilizers, and other drugs, overeating, taking the focus off yourself by picking a fight or arguing with others, or sexually acting out. (A quick romantic involvement with a new person in the aftermath of a divorce may be a temporary distraction from inner feelings of sadness and loss.)

Body

Physical changes are a natural part of emotional responses (increased blood pressure, insomnia, tension headaches, fatigue). When people go to great extremes to avoid feeling inner emotions and, in essence, grit their teeth, a common result is the emergence of stress-related physical symptoms. These symptoms can range from discomfort and annoyance to life-threatening conditions (severe high blood pressure, heart attacks, etc.).

Mind

The final major outlet for emotional pain is in the mind, experienced either as *feelings* or as *thoughts*. Those who notice mainly inner **feelings** may find that powerful emotions erupt: waves of sadness, panicky feelings, outbursts of anger. Those who are aware mainly of their inner **thoughts** typically experience continual fretting, recurrent painful memories, and/or worries about possible future calamities.

If the only way to deal with emotional pain is through distracting actions or by stressing your body, it's likely you won't fully heal from emotionally painful events, and that you'll continue to hurt on a deep inner level. If you're carrying a burden of unresolved distress it's hard to truly heal emotional problems.

Most therapists agree that our best shot at emotional healing and resolution lies in facing the reality of painful feelings, the truth of inner emotions, and processing the experiences through the mind (assessing inner feelings *and* thoughts). We'll explore more about how this is done shortly.

We've found it helpful to talk about two different kinds of emotional pain: "necessary pain" and "unnecessary pain." *Necessary pain* is basic, common, honest human anguish virtually anyone would feel when they encounter a tough life event, like the loss of a child, being fired, going through a divorce, major surgery. If you get burned, it hurts. You have little choice but to feel the pain. Certain life events just hurt.

> Most therapists agree that our best shot at emotional healing lies in facing the reality of painful events and processing the experiences . . .

Unnecessary pain is suffering that goes beyond the core emotional response. It is exaggerated, intensified, and prolonged suffering that, generally, is due to extremely self-critical thinking. In the wake of a seriously distressing personal event, many people launch into a ruthless attack on the self, either with actual statements spoken aloud to others or with private inner thoughts and beliefs. Examples of this include, "I'm so stupid," "I'm so screwed up," "Nothing I do is right," "What the hell is wrong with me?!" "I'm being silly and childish to feel so upset about this," "I hate myself."

An almost constant inner barrage of self-condemning thoughts represents one of the most common sources of human emotional suffering. While facing the truth of necessary pain is probably essential to successful emotional healing, unnecessary pain only intensifies and prolongs suffering.

One way to distinguish between necessary and unnecessary pain is to ask some basic questions: Even though this emotional pain hurts a lot, is it understandable? Does it make sense to me that I'm feeling this way given the fact that I'm going through a very stressful time in my life? Does this pain lead me to take corrective action? Does expressing the pain result in any sense of relief/release? Does it bring me closer with loved ones?

Of course, these are difficult questions to answer with certainty, since a good deal of necessary pain initially hurts so much that it's hard to imagine that it can serve any helpful purpose.

As one client put it, "For a long time after my divorce, I kept saying to myself, 'You've gotta get over this!' ... But eventually it dawned on me ... how is a person supposed to feel after her husband leaves her?! Of course, this hurts like hell. It's normal to feel upset."

An important facet of most courses of brief therapy is to help you sort through inner feelings and thoughts ... to confront, feel, acknowledge your legitimate necessary pain, while learning effective ways to stem the tide of inner self-criticism. (We'll talk a lot about strategies for reducing self-criticism in chapter 12.)

Chapter 8

From Talk That Hurts to Talk That Heals

Hᴏᴡ ᴄᴀɴ ᴛᴀʟᴋɪɴɢ help?

Good question. You may be thinking, "I've already talked about this problem a lot ... What good will it do to go in and talk to a shrink about it?" or "I've talked this to death ... I don't see how talking about it again will help me."

Let's be clear, *some types of talking aren't helpful* and, in fact, some kinds of talking about emotionally difficult issues can increase your despair and may make matters worse! So to begin our understanding of how talk therapy works and how it can help, let's consider three types of talking: talk that hurts, talk that hides, and—in the next chapter—talk that heals.

Talk That Hurts

It's worth repeating: some kinds of talking, about emotionally difficult issues, can increase despair and just make matters worse! Three very common kinds of talking that often occur during stressful times virtually guarantee you'll suffer even more. Talk like this (whether it's actually spoken aloud or just "self-talk" in your head) works like a pain amplifier, turning up the volume on the intensity of emotional pain.

The first hurtful style is *making extremely derogatory and critical comments about yourself.* We spoke about this in chapter 7 as a source of unnecessary pain.

A second form of hurtful talk is *jumping to inaccurate or unrealistic conclusions.* Such conclusions may suggest extreme calamities ("I'm falling apart . . . I am *completely* out of control!") or all-or-none statements ("Absolutely nothing I do is right!"). You may be making some poor decisions or mistakes, but you're certainly not 100 percent wrong about everything. This kind of talk just intensifies your idea that you are helpless and powerless—it's like throwing gasoline on your "distress fire."

The third common self-disturbing talk is *making extremely negative predictions.* For example, concluding that the very worst possible outcome *absolutely* will happen ("I'll never get over the sadness of this divorce!" or "I'll never find someone to love").

When these types of talking dominate, then in a real sense, talking does not help (we will share with you ways to actively change these kinds of negative self-talk in Chapters 12 and 17).

Talk That Hides

Many kinds of talk also take people far away from their honest inner emotions. Language can help us avoid or distort the truth. Let's look at several examples.

Quick Closure
"Yes, I know it's bad, but I'll get over it . . . Did you see the NBA playoff game last night?"

Minimizing
"Oh, it's not that bad."
"Other people have gone through worse things, I shouldn't complain."

"I feel sad, but I'm okay. I can handle it."

Injunctions

"I need to be strong."

"I shouldn't cry."

"I can't get so emotional . . . I've got to get myself under control."

Outright Denial

"I'm not upset. I'm . . . (sob) . . . okay."

In each of these statements, the words (or inner thoughts) direct your focus away from inner emotions or awareness of painful realities. This process can be temporarily helpful, especially when you're feeling overwhelmed. These natural human maneuvers are designed to protect us from too much pain. But this defensive stance can backfire and result in excessive blocking of honest emotions. Healing is stopped in its tracks.

So how can talking help you heal?

Sometimes it seems we talk ourselves into emotional difficulty. Can we also talk ourselves out of it?

Only if we're really careful about *how* we talk . . .

Talk That Heals

Talking out loud about important thoughts, feelings, and experiences can be one of the most effective and rapid ways to get clear about your emotions—unless of course it's the sort of talk we discussed in the previous chapter. If talking is done in a safe and supportive relationship with a therapist, the chances are excellent that it can lead to healing.

An emotional crisis can bring on lots of vague, ill-defined, disturbing emotions and sensations. It's easy to feel confused and unclear during these times. You may notice an intense uneasiness or tension in your body, a lump in your throat or tightness in your stomach. The confusing mix of emotions may only intensify anxiety, uncertainty, and helplessness.

If you're able to talk with an understanding person about your thoughts, feelings, and experiences, life often starts to make sense, bit by bit. You make connections between events and your feelings. It's as if you're shining a light into a dark cellar, gradually seeing clearly what's inside.

Most people don't like feeling uncertain and confused. As we gain clarity and understanding, we feel a greater sense of mastery and control. Talking—describing your emotions—often makes vague feelings concrete, and can help you understand them better.

Shawna's situation offers an example. She feels distant and alone in her marriage, as Tim has become increasingly preoccupied with work. The intimacy in their relationship has evaporated, causing her to feel sad and lonely. Here's a sample dialogue from one of her therapy sessions:

Shawna   Today at work for no reason, I started crying. It was crazy. Nothing bad happened. What's wrong with me?

Therapist   Well, let's look at what was happening today. What went on in the office?

Shawna   Nothing really.

Therapist   Well, maybe it will help if we go over it together. Tell me about today.

Shawna   I was at work. My girlfriend, Diane, was talking about her love relationship and how it wasn't working out. She's talked about it before, but all of a sudden for no reason, I just started feeling terrible. I felt like I was going to cry ... I'm not at all interested in her love life ...

Therapist   You were starting to cry?

Shawna   Yeah. (*She looks sad.*)

Therapist   I wonder if there was something about your conversation with her that struck a chord within you ... Tell me what comes to your mind.

Shawna   Well, I guess I thought, "Yeah, I know how you feel ... Things never work out for me either. I'm married and I'm unhappy." *(She starts to cry.)*

Therapist   That hurts ... Do your tears make sense?

Shawna   Yes.

In a brief interchange about the events of the day, the meaning and source of Shawna's pain became clear to her. This is not a fancy psychotherapeutic technique nor is it magical. People help other people do this sort of thing all the time: one person listens and encourages another person to talk. Many therapists take this approach: "Let's see what's happened ... I bet we can make sense of this." By *asking questions*, by *listening* and *encouraging discussion*, the therapist helps the client become aware of the personal meaning of events and emotions.

If the therapist had said, "I'm sure it was nothing," or "Well, you're over it now," or "It was probably just PMS," the process would have been quickly ended. Shawna would be just as much in the dark as before the session.

Shawna had initially tried to close the door by answering "Nothing really," to the therapist's inquiry, "Can you tell me what went on in the office?" The therapist nudged it open again, and she started to talk.

This is not just talking or "chitchat." The goal is speaking out loud with another toward understanding, discovering true feelings, and finding out what's really important. In this case, Shawna's sadness and confusion were replaced with greater understanding. As she became more aware of her own emotional turmoil, her feelings of sadness became an important issue for her to explore.

The talking helped Shawna open emotional doors, get in touch with her true feelings, understand herself better, view reality clearly. Her choices and actions won't always turn out right, but they'll be more in sync with her genuine needs, beliefs, and values. This gives her the best shot at emotional health.

More Ways Talk Can Help

In times of emotional distress, you may take things personally, quickly arrive at broad conclusions, and fail to notice important details. This can lead to lots of errors.

Let's listen to Mitch, a twenty-one-year-old college student, in conversation with his therapist:

Mitch   I was talking with my mother on the phone last night, trying to tell her about breaking up with Shelley. By the time I got off the phone, I felt terrible. I don't know, I just have a hard time getting along with my mom. Other people seem to have a good connection with their parents. What's wrong with me?

Let's take a closer look for a moment. Mitch is upset, and the conversation with his mother left him feeling worse. Part of the upset is from the recent breakup of a romance, part of it is from his disappointment about the phone conversation, but most of it comes from his belief about himself ("What is wrong with me?").

Mitch's therapist asked him to tell the story again, but to give more specifics. Mitch responded, "There's not much more to say. I felt lousy after the call, and that's that.

Mitch is doing what many of us do: he comes up with a fairly brief version of an event (a version that may neglect or ignore important elements). Let's see how the therapist helps Mitch to talk about this event in a different way.

Therapist   It sounds as though you felt really disappointed after talking with your mom.

Mitch   Right.

Therapist   I'd like to ask you to tell me about it again, but this time, slow down ... take your time. Share with me some more details. Okay?

Mitch	... Uh, okay ... (long pause). I said to her that Shelley had just told me she'd gone out with another guy ... and it just tore me up to hear that.
Therapist	What did your mom say to you then?
Mitch	*(pauses)* ... She said "Well, son, these things happen. You'll get over it." And then she sorta changed the subject.
Therapist	Well, how was that for you to hear?
Mitch	I guess she's right ...
Therapist	Well, maybe, but I want to ask you, at that moment when she said "these things happen," how did you feel? ... What did you notice in that moment?
Mitch	*(pauses)* ... I felt real let down, real sad.
Therapist	Why do you think? ... What was it in her words that might have touched on a feeling with you?
Mitch	I was calling to get support ... I wanted her to know how upset and sad I've been ...
Therapist	You wanted her to be there for you.
Mitch	Yeah ... and this has happened before with her. She just doesn't listen. Oh, she says she cares, but sometimes I wonder.
Therapist	You were reaching out to her and telling her about your feelings ... and she didn't really hear you?
Mitch	Not at all ... She was acting like it was no big deal ... but it is a big deal! This is probably the worst time of my life and she doesn't get it!
Therapist	You said at the end of the phone call you thought, "What's wrong with me?" What are you thinking right now?
Mitch	I don't think there's anything actually wrong with me, I think I was mostly upset because she didn't seem to hear me ... or to care.

What's really going on here in this two-minute dialogue? Initially, Mitch thought the problem was *him*. He had a negative view of himself: "Something's wrong with me." He's lost Shelley, he isn't communicating with his mother, and he's down on himself. The therapist's encouragement helped Mitch to slow down and talk about the events as they unfolded, and to notice how he felt. In Mitch's conversation with his therapist he was able to increase his awareness, pay attention to, notice, and acknowledge his emotional reactions. And he explored the *personal meaning* of the event—what losing Shelley *meant* to him.

As Mitch became clearer about what actually happened during the conversation with his mother, and how he really felt, he changed his view of himself. This is a very important change. His self-perception shifted from "There must be something wrong with me" to "I was sad, I was reaching out. It's understandable for someone at a time like this to look for support. It's not so much that there is something wrong with me. It's that my mother was unable or unwilling to really hear my pain."

Mitch has a lot of sadness and grief. He doesn't need to increase his distress by making unrealistic negative assumptions about himself. Unlike talking with his mother, talking with his therapist helped turn around his attitude toward himself.

Talking like this—exploring events realistically, clarifying feelings, gaining understanding—is a powerful way to change your view of a situation and can significantly reduce unnecessary pain. This is talk that heals, and paves the way for positive attitudes and actions in your life.

Chapter 9

From Illusion
to Reality

REALITY FOR EACH of us is influenced by what other people tell us: "Your father is a good man." "You know, your mother really does love you." "I really want to spend more time with you, honey, but I have a lot of work to do." "I'm doing this for your own good." "Of course I love you. I don't have to *tell* you . . . you should *know* it!"

Views of reality are also shaped by injunctions: "Don't rock the boat," "Don't be so sensitive," "I should like my job; it pays well," "I shouldn't complain; others have it a lot worse than I do."

Some mental health professionals believe that this kind of thinking occurs in the conscious and logical part of the mind. This external view of reality (beliefs told to you by others) tends to dominate conscious awareness and constitutes what we will call "Version One" of reality. Sometimes Version One may be accurate; sometimes not.

On another level, we may perceive, think about, and respond to the world in a very different way. This level is based more on direct personal experience, intuitions, sensations and feelings—a more immediate, gut-level response to what's happening in the moment. These perceptions and responses have little to do with what we have been told by others to think or believe. Rather they come naturally from within the self—a type of inner truth. We refer to this internal view as "Version Two."

Versions One and Two may differ. Years ago, during her first menstrual period, Beth complained to her mother of pain-

"Version One" of reality (beliefs told to you by others) tends to dominate conscious awareness . . . "Version Two" is based on direct personal experiences, intuitions, feelings.

ful cramping. Her mother responded, "You're too young to have a period!" The young girl was now confronted with conflicting views of reality: Mom's view ("You are not having a period") and her own view ("I hurt"). A self-confident child might say, "Mom, you're wrong!" but many children will accept their mother's version of truth, and ignore the reality of their own experience.

The internal reality of physical pain, emotions and needs can be ignored by thinking things like: "I'm making a big deal out of nothing," or "It's not that bad," or "Mom must know what's really happening." Or you can deny your feelings by blocking them from awareness—either partially or completely—leaving you out of touch with your inner reality.

Recall Shawna's story from the previous chapter. At first she didn't even notice her anger toward Tim. She just felt upset, afraid and tearful. For her, Version One meant, "Tim is a good man. He says he loves me. It could be worse." In therapy she began to listen more carefully to her inner experience, and gradually became aware of her Version Two: "He's rarely at home. There is little intimacy. I feel empty, unhappy, and angry. He says 'I love you,' but his behavior tells a different story."

Discovering the truth about her relationship with Tim brought Shawna closer to objective reality. Though she knew Version One was fashioned on empty promises, words, and her own strong hopes, she wanted desperately to believe it. But it wasn't true. As she talked and explored her feelings since beginning therapy sessions, Version One faded and gave way to her real feelings. Tim may have had good intentions and sincerely believed that his words and promises of love were genuine. However, the bottom-line reality for Shawna was Version Two. She didn't like it, and it hurt, but it was real.

Check It Out!

Here are a couple of "reality checks" you can do to promote your own growth and emotional healing:

- *Question your own personal Version Ones views of important others* (parents, spouses, relatives, friends), *world views* ("The world is fair," "Bad things don't happen to good people"), and *guidelines for living* ("Don't be emotional," "Don't be so sensitive," "Don't get angry").

- Pay *attention to your direct experience*—inner reactions, sensation, longings, and emotions. Don't deny what you know is true.

  Facing the truth often means pain . . .
  But doing so allows you to heal and grow!

"The Truth Shall Make You Free"

The Biblical saying is proven every day by patients in therapy. Your truth cannot be defined or dictated from without, but must be discovered from within. Brief therapy can help.

When you make time to really talk about your thoughts, feelings, and other inner experiences, one outcome is often an increased awareness of inner truths. "My childhood was not happy." "My father didn't truly show me love." "My job isn't gratifying." "My mother hurt me." "I feel a lack of closeness in my marriage." Such discoveries both hurt and help. You must face and grieve the loss of illusions (for example, the illusion of a happy childhood or a meaningful marriage).

Ultimately, Version Two may be okay. You may start to see your partner for who they really are. Maybe that's all right, maybe not. Accurate awareness may ignite open conflict or promote problem solving in a relationship; it can lead to marital counseling or even to divorce. But increased awareness of inner truths may result in less confusion and a stronger sense of self.

Within each person there are many "truths," so the approach is not aimed at finding "one truth," but the discovery of all your beliefs, needs, and emotions. It's a lifelong process. As you begin to clarify these aspects of yourself, you can sort out who you are, figure out what problems you want to tackle, and feel more solid about the actions you choose to take.

Brief therapy may be your most valuable resource as you find your way.

From Isolation
to Contact

SHARED PAIN IS easier to bear.

Well now, that depends on how your sharing is received by others. Sometimes opening up to another person can make matters worse, as is the case when the other person responds to the expression of emotion by *judging*. In contrast, sharing when responded to with *acceptance* and *support* can contribute much to the healing process. In this chapter we'll take a look at some helpful and some not-so-helpful conditions for sharing your pain.

Good Therapists Don't Judge

They do, however, offer honest feedback ... and a trained therapist knows the difference.

Friends sometimes will judge your feelings or actions in the name of "honest feedback." Their intentions may be constructive, but the result can be very destructive. Sometimes such judging is blatant; sometimes it is subtle, but it's almost never helpful.

Let's look at some examples:

Obvious Judgment

"You should be ashamed of yourself."

"You're being too emotional, too sensitive."

Disguised Judgment

"Now, now, don't cry."

"Look on the bright side."

"You need to put it behind you and get on with your life."

The obvious or underlying message implied is judgment: "It's wrong to feel that way" or "There is something wrong with you." In response, the person in pain may begin to feel ashamed or inadequate, and shut down emotionally. She is likely to become increasingly inhibited about sharing her inner feelings, further cutting her off from connections with others. In such cases, sharing is hurtful rather than healing.

Other Types of Nonhelpful Sharing

Some listeners can't wait to jump in and offer brilliant insights or good advice. Sometimes this response is helpful, but often it is not. In fact, it generally closes the door to deeper emotional sharing.

Other listeners will attempt to convince you—and themselves—that they understand. True understanding is hard to achieve. When the listener quickly, or in a phony, shallow way says, "I understand," it's usually a type of non-helpful sharing. People are so unique and so complex in their makeup that to come even close to a state of true understanding requires a lot of listening and a good deal of time spent coming to know the other person. The friend who says, "I understand," is probably trying to be helpful and trying to express care and

"It takes two to speak the truth—one to speak and another to hear."

—Henry David Thoreau

concern. However, the person sharing her pain often thinks, "How can she really understand?" The result again is a closing down of emotions and a reluctance to share.

Brief therapy offers a safe place to share emotional experiences and feelings with another person in a nonjudgmental and supportive atmosphere.

Benefits of Positive Sharing

When sharing pain with another person, you may experience strong emotions that otherwise would seem completely overwhelming. The other person can be like an anchor, providing some degree of stability and strength, lessening the intensity of your emotions.

A crisis may call up a host of emotions, some too intense, some too shameful to handle alone. An extremely valuable consequence of having the opportunity to discuss your feelings with a therapist is feeling okay about having human emotions. As a person listens to and accepts you, you may begin to feel less guilt, less shame, and disturbing emotions begin to seem normal and understandable. Many people are afraid that others will be disgusted, shocked, or critical when they reveal deep inner feelings. But a tremendous sense of relief can result when you see that another person hears you and does not condemn you.

Sharing pain with another also gives you a chance to talk out loud about your feelings. We discussed the value of talking in Chapter 8. People can, and do, talk to themselves, of course, but talking is more effective when another person listens. It's an easier way to notice more clearly just what you're thinking, and how you're feeling.

Finally, and very importantly, sharing allows you simply to *be with another human being during a time of distress*. Most people feel any life crisis more acutely in isolation. Being in contact with a therapist, a close friend, loved one—even a stranger who is a good listener—can be soothing and healing.

Sharing pain connects us to one another. Compassion and love play an important role in the healing process.

Finally . . .

Brief psychotherapy isn't just talk, or chitchat. It's not hand-holding or an emotional crutch. It is important, emotionally difficult work, and a serious endeavor. Psychotherapy, when the chemistry is right between client and therapist, helps people help themselves during hard times. Therapy is no longer seen so much as a cure for emotional illness as it is an effective way to facilitate growth, encourage effective coping, and provide support when life is hard. Ultimately, psychotherapy works only when it helps people find their own strength.

Chapter 11

Disorders Responsive to Specific Treatments

IN RECENT YEARS mental health professionals have made great strides in the development of specific therapies for the treatment of a number of psychological disorders. These approaches (outlined below) include both psychological therapies and medical treatments that have been shown to be effective in carefully conducted research. For many years, some therapists have, unfortunately, made unsubstantiated claims that their particular brand of therapy was effective and often times boasted that their approach was good for "everything that ails you." We feel strongly that potential psychotherapy clients are on much more solid ground when they seek out therapeutic approaches that have documented effectiveness.

It must be made clear that research studies are conducted with large groups of people, and even when a particular treatment is shown to be effective (or superior to other approaches) this certainly does not mean that all people treated by that approach experience substantial improvement. Even with the most tried and true treatments, some people may have a less than desirable outcome. Be that as it may, the potential therapy client who is well informed is clearly in a better position to know which approaches are most likely to successfully address their unique problems or concerns.*

In discussing specific treatments, we will first describe and define those disorders for which specific treatments have been developed. This will be followed in each case by a brief description of those therapies that have been shown to be effective.

Depression

Depression can present in a number of different ways, but most people suffering from depression experience some of the following symptoms:

- Mood changes: sadness, despair, or irritability
- Lack of vitality, enthusiasm, and motivation
- Difficulties with concentration and forgetfulness
- Physical complaints:
  - Weight gain or weight loss
  - Insomnia or excessive sleeping
  - Loss of sexual desire
  - Exhaustion and fatigue
  - Occasionally, intense restlessness
- Suicidal ideas
- Feelings of powerlessness or hopelessness
- Feelings of worthlessness or low self-esteem

Psychotherapies

Cognitive Therapy (Beck 1976). In depression it is common for people to perceive the world in extremely negative and pessimistic ways. Your view of others, the future, and

---

* For a comprehensive discussion of psychological treatments and research on effectiveness, please see *What You Can Change ... and What You Can't*, by Martin E. P. Seligman, Ph.D., New York, Fawcett Columbine Publishers, 1993.

yourself tend to accentuate what is inadequate, bleak, or tragic. This leads to a pervasive, depressive, and hopeless view of the world. In cognitive therapy the therapist actively works with the client to help him or her to spot negative thinking and to challenge it (to engage in more accurate and realistic thinking and perceiving). This is done not only in therapy sessions, but also by way of between-session homework projects. Cognitive therapy is an active and directive form of psychotherapy that has been shown to be very effective in treating mild to moderately severe depression.

Behavior Therapy (Lewinshon 1984). Behavior therapy for depression focuses largely on encouraging clients to become more active in social and recreational events. Depression often results in marked social withdrawal, and as a consequence, depressed people become progressively cut off from meaningful and enjoyable life activities. The theory is that diminished positive experiences can significantly increase depressive symptoms. And research has demonstrated that when people are involved in a program that pushes them to get active, this alone can often reduce depressive symptoms. This approach is helpful for people suffering with mild-to-moderate depression.

Interpersonal Therapy (Klerman and Weissman 1984). Interpersonal therapy (IPT) is derived from the observation that a common source of distress and depression emanates from problematic or dysfunctional relationships. In IPT clients are taught how to develop effective skills for communication and problem solving. Often this includes therapy sessions that involve the client and significant others (spouse or the entire family). IPT has also been shown to be quite effective in treating mild to moderately severe depression.

Biological Approaches

1. Antidepressant medication is quite effective for the treatment of moderate to severe depression (see chapter 18).

2. Excessive alcohol consumption is a common *cause* of depression (it can have a devastating effect on brain

functioning), therefore **reducing or eliminating alcohol consumption** can be a very effective approach to treating depression. (Note: If alcohol use is excessive, discontinuation should always be medically supervised. Acute alcohol withdrawal can be dangerous.)

3. Regular exercise and moderate **exposure to bright light** (for example, daylight for about one hour a day) have been shown to be helpful in treating some forms of depression.

4. Severe depression can be successfully treated by **electroconvulsive therapy** (ECT).

Panic Disorder

Recurring episodes of intense anxiety that come on suddenly, rapidly escalate to a level of panic, and usually subside within five to twenty minutes. During such "attacks" people may experience many of the following symptoms:

- Trembling, nervousness, panic
- Shortness of breath and a smothering sensation
- Rapid heartbeat, lightheadedness, dizziness
- A sense of impending doom or the belief that one is either "going crazy" or about to die
- After a number of such attacks, people often develop phobias (for example, a fear of crowds, fear of driving, fear of being away from home)

Psychotherapies

Cognitive Therapy (Beck and Emery 1985). Often during the first moments of a panic attack, as the person begins to notice some physical symptoms, the mind becomes flooded with "catastrophic thoughts." These generally are highly emotionally charged conclusions such as "Oh, my God, I'm having a heart attack!" or "I feel like I am going crazy." These thoughts, in a powerful way, actually throw gas on the fire. Such conclusions (as natural as they may be when one is feeling panic) scare people and intensify the attack. In cognitive therapy for panic attacks, the therapist helps the client learn to use calming and realistic thinking (self-talk) in place of catastrophic thinking. One example would be to actively tell oneself, "This is a panic attack . . . It's very uncomfortable, but not dangerous . . . Also I know that these attacks usually last only a few minutes . . . Hang in there, and it will pass soon." Cognitive therapy (especially when combined with interoceptive therapy and breathing techniques—outlined below) has been shown to be very effective in the treatment of panic disorder.

Interoceptive Therapy is taught after the client has learned some basic cognitive approaches (as outlined above). In interoceptive therapy, the therapist works with the client during sessions to actually create some physical symptoms that the client typically experiences during panic attacks. For example, shortness of breath can be brought on by one minute of rapid breathing, or a racing heart can be provoked by running up and down a flight of stairs. Such physical symptoms typically cause a person with panic disorder to feel uneasy and frightened. But by inducing them intentionally, and then using calming and realistic "self-talk," clients can often quickly learn to gain mastery over the symptoms (rather than have the symptoms lead to fear and an escalation of panic). Interoceptive therapy paired with cognitive therapy is even more effective than cognitive therapy alone.

Graded Exposure: If phobias have developed then a technique called graded exposure (also referred to as systematic desensitization) is the treatment of choice (Wolpe and Wolpe 1988; Beck and Emery 1985). This approach however, is only effective once panic attacks have been nearly or completely alleviated (with psychotherapy and/or medication treatment, addressed below). Since graded exposure is a technique useful with other anxiety disorders, it is described in detail below.

Graded Exposure

When people have developed specific fears or anxieties (for example, fear of heights, fear of public speaking, social anxiety, or phobias developed in the midst of panic disorder), graded exposure is often the treatment of choice. Here is how it works: Central to all fears and phobias are three features, (1) intense discomfort or anxiety, (2) feelings of being powerless or out of control, and (3) a strong urge to avoid the situation provoking the fear. To overcome such fears, it is important to first develop some anxiety management techniques. These may include reassuring "self-talk," relaxation, eye movement, and breathing techniques. Such techniques are taught during therapy sessions and practiced again and again until the client has mastered them.

Phase two of graded exposure involves establishing a *fear hierarchy*. The therapist and client will together develop a list of fearful situations that begin with low-level stressors and progress up to situations that are likely to be experienced as very frightening. Following is an example of a person who has developed a fear of driving her car.

Example Hierarchy

1. Getting in the car and sitting in the driveway with the engine off

2. Turning on the engine, leaving the car in park, then turning the engine off

3. Backing car onto street in front of home, then driving back into driveway

4. Driving down the street in front of home and then returning home

5. Driving around the block in the neighborhood

6. Driving two blocks away from home and back

7. Driving to a local store, but using back streets (not the freeway)

8. Driving on a major street to a local shopping mall

9. Driving on a freeway but not during rush hours

10. Driving on a busy freeway at rush hour and changing lanes

Such a hierarchy is made up of a progressive situation ranging on a scale from 1 to 10.

Phase three of graded exposure simply involves taking level one of the hierarchy and vividly imagining it during a therapy session. If any anxiety is experienced, the therapist, acting like a coach, helps the client use anxiety-management skills to reduce the feeling of anxiety. This is repeated, if necessary, until the client feels confident in his or her ability to reduce emotional distress. The next step may involve going into the real situation described in hierarchy level one (a relatively low-stress situation) and again, if anxiety is experienced, using techniques to reduce distress. Movement to the next most stressful situation only occurs as the client has come to feel confident in his or her ability to manage anxiety.

At the heart of graded exposure is the acquisition of effective anxiety-management skills and the experience of an increased sense of mastery and self-confidence in approaching the feared situation. This behavioral approach is highly effective in the treatment of many different types of fears and phobias.

Biological Approaches

1. Breathing techniques: Often in the opening moments of a panic attack, breathing becomes abnormal (either rapid shallow breathing and/or sighing). Both of these patterns of breathing produce the following symptoms: light headedness, dizziness, and shortness of breath or a smothering sensation. These symptoms are understandably very distressing. However, some very simple breath-

ing techniques have been shown to be highly effective in controlling these respiration-related anxiety symptoms and generally are approaches taught to people suffering from panic and other anxiety disorders. Breathing techniques fall into two categories. The first is recommended if symptoms of anxiety are just starting to occur and are mild. The technique involves taking a normal breath (*not* shallow, *not* deep) and then *slowly* exhaling through pursed lips, as if you were going to whistle. This type of breathing should continue until the anxiety completely subsides, which may take several minutes.

Technique number two is to be used if anxiety symptoms have become intense and one is experiencing noticeable lightheadedness/shortness of breath. The client is taught how to breathe in and out, repeatedly, into a paper bag or other small, enclosed space (paper lunch bag, empty Kleenex box, or head under the covers). This approach, when used until all anxiety symptoms disappear, helps to restore normal levels of blood gases in circulation, and is remarkably effective in quickly reducing anxiety symptoms.

2. Elimination or reduction of substances: Caffeine, decongestants, and alcohol are known to increase panic symptoms.

3. Antianxiety and antidepressant medication: can be highly effective in treating panic disorder (see chapter 18).

Generalized Anxiety Disorder (GAD)

GAD is a form of chronic anxiety; the person feels anxious or tense almost every day. This is not in response to specific stressful events. Rather the GAD sufferer finds that every day events trigger continuous anxiety. Unlike panic disorder, people with GAD rarely or never experience full-blown panic attacks; however, they may suffer from the following symptoms:

- Tension or nervousness
- Exaggerated sensitivity to low-level stresses
- Physical complaints: tension headaches, insomnia, gastrointestinal distress, muscle tension
- Fatigue
- Feeling on guard or apprehensive

The hallmark of GAD is **worry** (fretting, anticipating bad or troublesome events, self-doubting). GAD often begins in adolescence or early adulthood and may last a lifetime if untreated.

There is some evidence to suggest that one aspect of GAD is hypersensitivity or chronic over-arousal of the stress-response system in the body (brain and sympathetic nervous system).

Psychotherapies

Anxiety-management techniques have been developed that are often very helpful in reducing chronic anxiety. These include the following approaches:

a. **Cognitive therapy**: The focus of cognitive therapy for GAD includes: (1) *Risk assessment*: systematic assessment of likely risks involved in everyday situations (this can help to counter the tendency to anticipate disaster or catastrophes). It encourages willful, conscious, and rational assessment of potential risks as well as an evaluation of the likelihood that negative outcomes will occur (a person may worry, "If I contradict my boss, I'll get fired"), and the anticipation of this outcome generates anxiety. On closer examination, the person may develop clarity about the objective realities, (other employees have contradicted the boss and no one has been fired). (2) Worry often occurs in an automatic and unexamined way. Cognitive approaches also involve techniques designed to help people more consciously evaluate stressful situations. For example, keeping a "worry record," scheduling "worry time" to devote to careful assessment and reflection about stresses. (Instead of ongoing or continuous worry that occurs in an automatic and habitual way, setting aside twenty to thirty minutes a day to intentionally worry often, paradoxically, reduces generalized anxiety. (3) *Problem solving*: specific approaches to problem solving have been developed that often result in people feeling less anxious and in more control. Such techniques are often taught and practiced as a part of cognitive therapy.

b. **Decreasing physiological arousal**: Three techniques have been found to be effective in reducing physical symptoms of anxiety. These include relaxation training (see page 110), meditation, and eye-movement techniques (see page 121).

c. **Exposure therapy**: Once anxiety management techniques have been mastered, clients are encouraged to approach certain situations in their daily lives that have, in the past, been sources of significant anxiety. They then use learned techniques to reduce anxiety. Repeated success with *exposure* eventually leads to increased feelings of self-confidence and a reduction in anxiety.

Biological Approaches

1. A program of regular exercise (moderate exertion is okay, aerobic-level is better) has been shown to consistently reduce generalized anxiety

2. Eliminating substances that increase anxiety such as caffeine and decongestants can often make for a remarkable decrease in generalized anxiety

3. Medical treatment for GAD may include the use of certain antidepressants (Paxil, Prozac, Zoloft, Celexa, or Serzone) and/or the nonaddictive tranquilizer Buspar.

Social Phobia/Social Anxiety

Intense uneasiness in social situations or while interacting with others is one of the most common anxiety disorders. This typically leads one to avoid social gatherings and may result in leading an isolated or lonely lifestyle.

Psychotherapies

Anxiety management and graded exposure: The client and therapist discuss in some detail those situations that provoke anxiety. Then the client is taught anxiety-reduction techniques (see page 75–76) followed by graded exposure. Such approaches are most successful if accompanied by the acquisition of assertive skills (see below) and rehearsal in a supportive group setting.

Assertiveness training: This is a specific type of therapy geared to teach clients a set of interpersonal interactions and communication skills. This can be accomplished in individual therapy, but is probably best when done in the context of a group. In **group therapy** assertive skills are discussed, modeled, and rehearsed within a supportive and encouraging setting. At some point clients begin practicing assertive behavior outside of therapy, in real life situations, in a graded exposure fashion (first tackling rather low risk/low stress situations, and with increasing success and mastery, approaching more problematic interactions). With repeated experiences and mastery, anxiety often subsides significantly.

Biological Approaches

Psychiatric medications that have been shown to be effective in treating some forms of social phobia include

- Antidepressants: especially those that affect the neuro-chemical serotonin—Prozac, Paxil, Celexa, Serzone, Zoloft

- MAO-inhibitors: Nardil or Parnate

- Beta blockers: Inderal

- Minor tranquilizers: Ativan or Xanax

Post-Traumatic Stress Disorder (PTSD)

This disorder is often seen in the aftermath of exposure to a very frightening event (being raped, almost being killed, witnessing the death of another person, being in a natural disaster or a combat situation). Common symptoms may include:

- Vivid re-experiencing of the traumatic event in thoughts, memories, or nightmares

- Avoiding situations which remind one of the traumatic event

- Memory impairment (amnesia for the event)

- Odd feelings of detachment, numbness, or unreality

- Intense feelings of anxiety, irritability, depression, and/or exquisite emotional sensitivity

A central problem in PTSD is that people become afraid of their memories and the feelings that such memories evoke. They may also develop phobias and avoidance of situations that tend to trigger distressing memories.

(Please note: PTSD emerging in the aftermath of fairly recently occurring traumatic events may be treatable in brief therapy. A more severe form of PTSD attributable to severe early childhood trauma, abuse, or neglect generally requires long-term psychotherapy).

Psychotherapies

Ultimately, clients who suffer from PTSD must be able to face and talk about the tragic events and painful memories. However, it is essential that this be done in a way where the person re-experiences memories and emotions, but is not overwhelmed by them. One of the most important aspects of therapy for PTSD is to develop a sense of safety in the therapeutic relationship. An effective therapist can be with the client, can hear about horrible experiences, and maintain his or her own emotional sturdiness. The client can come to see and know that these things can be talked about, without "blowing away" the therapist. Well-trained therapists are able to listen and understand intense emotions while providing support.

Anxiety-management technique: An important aspect of treatment of PTSD is the restoration of a personal sense of control over intense emotions. Techniques such as cognitive therapy and eye-movement approaches (see page 121) are often quite helpful. One particular, specialized version of this is referred to as EMDR (eye movement desensitization and reprocessing [Shapiro 1995]).

Biological Approaches

Serotonin antidepressants (Prozac, Paxil, Celexa, Serzone, and Zoloft), generally prescribed in moderate-to-high doses, are quite helpful in providing clients with an enhanced capacity to maintain control over intense emotions.

Obsessive-Compulsive Disorder (OCD)

- Recurring, persistent, unpleasant or senseless thoughts or impulses which are difficult to prevent or ignore (constant worry about dirt and germs)

- Repetitive actions or rituals carried out in an attempt to reduce obsessive ideas (repeated hand washing, repeatedly checking and rechecking to make sure doors and windows are locked, constant attempts to keep one's home extremely neat and orderly)

Psychotherapies

Phase One: Exposure: The client is exposed to a feared situation. For example, if there is a fear of germs or contamination examples of exposure may be to remove garbage from a trashcan or to touch a toilet seat.

Phase Two: Response Prevention: Exposure typically results in significant distress, and is usually responded to by engaging in ritual behavior, such as repeated hand washing (which eventually helps to reduce anxiety). In this phase of treatment, the therapist helps to prevent the client from engaging in the anxiety-reducing ritual. Obviously, the initial result is considerable anxiety, although the therapist will make strong attempts to support and encourage the client to "hang in there." This part of the treatment continues for about forty-five minutes and then the session ends. The initial anxiety usually increases, but near the end of the session, many clients begin to notice anxiety subsiding. Typically this procedure is repeated a number of times (most often, requiring 18-20 sessions of exposure and response prevention).

Although this approach is initially difficult for clients to experience, after a number of sessions, they begin to feel an increasing sense of mastery, as they come to know that, almost invariably, with time intense anxiety subsides. Exposure and response prevention have been shown to yield very good results for most clients with OCD.

Biological Approaches

1. Serotonin antidepressants are effective in about 60 percent of people suffering from OCD (see chapter 18).

2. Severe OCD that does not respond to psychotherapy or medications may be treated by a specific neurosurgical procedure (cingulate bundle cut).

PART III

A Coping Skills Manual

"OKAY SO I'M NOT crazy, it just feels that way. What do I do now? All these self-help books are the same; they say I've already learned everything I need to know in kindergarten, I just have to use what I know. Well, I'm too tired to care. Tell me something I can do. I just don't think I can cope with all this."

Coping skills are not mysterious. Except for a few basic survival skills, you're not born with them—they're learned behaviors. Some people develop good coping and problem-solving skills early in life, but some of us weren't that lucky. Life is unpredictable, and while sometimes the path is smooth and silky, most of us find a few rocks in the path from time to time and an occasional avalanche or two.

In this section of the book we will be sharing with you some specific guidelines for effective coping. These strategies have been developed and refined by mental health professionals over the past two decades. Your therapist will probably introduce one or more of them as a part of your treatment. If not, we think you'll find them valuable self-help resources to complement and support your brief therapy.

Nothing fancy here; just solid action plans that can make a difference for people who are under stress. We'll focus on five areas: (1) *cognitive coping skills* ("cognitive" refers to perceptions and thoughts, thus this part will deal with ways to increase your ability to think clearly, problem-solve, and maintain a realistic perspective), (2) *interpersonal problem-solving and conflict resolution skills* (for effectively resolving difficulties with others), (3) *staying healthy/reducing stress* (keeping physically healthy can make a difference, especially during times of significant distress), (4) self-monitoring *homework* (active ways to monitor your progress), and (5) *strengthening your sense of self* (ways to feel more "solid" and self-confident).

These are skills almost anyone can develop, and they will help to lessen your emotional pain and give you back some sense of control over your feelings. They can increase the likelihood of success in brief therapy—and in your life beyond therapy.

Chapter 12

"I think I can . . .
I think I can . . . "

"**I** WANT TO GO back to school so I can get a better paying job. But my youngest is having problems; his grades are dropping and his attitude is getting worse and worse. His father is no help at all!"

Stephanie is a single mom with two teenage boys, working at a dead-end job that barely lets her pay the bills.

"*I don't have medical coverage and can't afford a therapist for us. What am I supposed to do?! I could quit my job and get on welfare, then at least I'd have some medical care. But I don't want to do that. I want to go to school, but then I'd have even less time with the boys and they really need me now.*"

We're going to let you choose Stephanie's next line. Does she say, "*I can't cope. I feel helpless . . . stuck, I can't deal with all this!*" Or, "*Things are really tough right now, but I've been through worse. This is going to be hard, but I can handle it*"?

Stephanie is, as the saying goes, "between a rock and a hard place." She knows she is facing a difficult time. However, if she *believes* she can cope, she may be distressed, but not overwhelmed—she'll feel more or less confident that she can manage.

On the other hand, if Stephanie begins to *think and believe,* "I can't cope," she'll feel more and more stress. Have her coping skills actually diminished? No. But her self-confidence is lessened if she doesn't believe she's able to handle the situation. Feelings of helplessness always increase distress.

How You Think Makes a Difference

We interpret our world through our *thoughts*, our *beliefs*, our *perceptions*, and our *attitudes*. By becoming aware of how your thoughts and attitudes influence your feelings, you can gain more control over your feelings—and your life.

Thoughts and attitudes are not mystical experiences. They naturally occur in our heads all the time—we're constantly "talking to myself," sometimes out loud, but more often silently. As we discussed before your "self-talk" includes your observations of the world, conclusions, predictions, and problem solving. It happens *automatically*. And that self-talk can actually create or intensify positive or negative *feelings* (sadness, self-doubt, depression, anxiety, fear, anger, pain, discomfort, uncertainty . . .).

When you're faced with serious stressors or traumatic events, your self-talk is likely to become more negative ("I can't cope . . . Everything I do is wrong"), leading to low self-esteem and lack of confidence.

Your life—and the progress of your brief therapy—will improve if you begin to turn your self-talk around. You can do that by paying attention to it, then taking action steps to change it.

Listen to Yourself

In order to get a handle on this thinking-feeling-action process, you'll need to start *paying attention* to what you are feeling and thinking. For example, you'll notice change in your moods and feelings during therapy sessions. Your therapist will help by asking questions about how you're feeling, and what you think or believe about an event or person or life circumstance. The goal will be to spot unrealistic, negative, or pessimistic thinking when it occurs.

As you begin to notice and recognize your thoughts and feelings you may actually find your feelings getting stronger. That's because for the first time in a long time you may actually be allowing yourself to feel them. Don't panic, it's normal!

How to Turn Your Negative Thinking Around

Please keep in mind that you don't have to change your whole personality to have an impact on negative thinking. All you have to do is a simple three-step process. It takes just a minute. *Step one*: Notice negative, automatic thoughts the moment they occur. Ask yourself, "I'm feeling upset right now . . . What's going through my mind? What am I thinking?" *Step two*: Ask yourself, "Are my thoughts at this moment 100 percent accurate and realistic?" *Step three*: Replace negative and/or unrealistic thoughts with thoughts that are more accurate. In the next few pages we'll elaborate on this simple process. Let's start by looking at an example.

> Your life—and the progress of your brief therapy—will improve if you can begin to turn your self-talk around.

Imagine you are asked to give a twenty-minute presentation at work before a group of fifty people. You seriously dislike speaking in public; in fact, it terrifies you. If you are like a lot of people, you may begin thinking, moments before you talk, "Oh my God, look at all those people, I'm going to blow it! I'm going to start to shake, my voice is going to crack, and I'll forget my speech. I'll humiliate myself and they're going to think I'm stupid!" These all-too-common thoughts are good examples of the sort of self-talk that focuses largely on negative outcomes. Such pessimism can scare you and increase the intensity of your experience to disaster, anxiety, and self-doubt.

If you were to think instead, "Oh my God, look at all those people. Now settle down. Sure I'm feeling anxious. Lots of people don't like public speaking and it's normal to be a little on edge about this, but I need to encourage and support myself. I'm going to give it my best. I may not win an Academy Award, but I'll get through this." Or, "I don't like this kind of stuff, but I'll survive. It may not be pleasant, but it won't kill me."

By replacing the negative thoughts with realistic, appropriate, and supportive beliefs, you admit to your unpleasant feelings while giving yourself support. In doing so, you are also stemming the tide of negative thoughts. The last thing that you need to do prior to getting up to give a talk is to scare yourself! The stress will not be completely avoided, but the outcome will be quite different. Your silent but potent inner voice can have a tremendous effect on the amount of stress you experience and your feelings of self-confidence.

Challenge Your Thinking

You're saying, "Okay. I can do that, but be more specific." Fair enough.

In this section, we've identified several common obstacles to healthy thinking and some specific ways to challenge them. You can interrupt negative thinking if you'll stop and ask yourself a question that examines your thoughts. Look inside yourself and bring your thoughts into conscious awareness. Use your realistic thinking to make positive thoughts and changes. The idea is to *identify* how your thoughts are upsetting you, then to *challenge* any faulty thinking and replace it with a healthier outlook. How many of these are part of your style?

- *Jumping to conclusions* ("I just know she thinks I'm a jerk," "I know I'm blowing this job interview ... the interviewer looks bored to tears"). How can anyone know with certainty what others are thinking or feeling? No one can read another person's mind. Jumping to negative conclusions always increases distress. In such situations, it's helpful to ask yourself, "What do I *really* know about this situation?"

- *Predicting the worst possible outcome* ("This is going to be *horrible!*" "I'll never get over it"). Remind yourself that you can't tell the future. Then ask yourself, "Where is the evidence that this terrible catastrophe is about to happen? What makes me think that this absolutely *will* happen?"

- *All-or-nothing thinking* ("I can't do *anything* right!"). Challenge directly with "Is that absolutely true? I can't do *anything* right?", then list a few things you've done correctly. Focus on the specific problem or mistake and acknowledge it.

- *Seeing the worst* (and ignoring the positive things). Remind yourself, "I need to look at the whole picture, including the good things, not just the things that go wrong." This is *not* a "just think positive" approach. We believe that such a sugar-coated view of things is not helpful or realistic. What we suggest is developing a reality-based and balanced perspective, considering both positive and negative realities.

- *Labeling* ("I'm an idiot"). You're not, or you wouldn't have come this far on your own. Like everybody else, you've done some dumb things in your life, and you will again. But "idiot" is a term with precise meaning (look it up). If you really were, you wouldn't be reading this book. Keep in mind that you are a person who makes human mistakes and is capable of human successes as well.

> This is *not* a "just think positive" approach. We believe that such a sugar-coated view of things is not helpful or realistic. What we suggest is developing a reality-based and balanced perspective, considering both positive and negative realities.

- *Self-blame* ("It's all my fault"). Under stress it's common to fall into excessive self-blame. But assuming 100 percent of the fault is probably not realistic and serves mainly to increase feelings of self-hatred and low self-esteem.

- *The "shoulds"* (believing firmly that you or others *should* or *must* act only a certain way). Tell yourself that many things happen that are not pleasant, but this doesn't mean that they "should" or "shouldn't" be. It may be helpful and less painful to rephrase your thoughts in terms of what you want (Instead of "She should know how I feel," say to yourself, "I want her to understand, but she can't read my mind." Or rephrase as "This shouldn't be happening," "It is happening and I don't like it")

  The "shoulds" are an especially powerful negative thought pattern. When you think with shoulds you view yourself as a victim. Feelings of powerlessness and help-lessness increase. Thinking with the shoulds is a way of strongly insisting that things must be a certain way. Thinking these thoughts never changes the reality—it only makes you feel worse.

  An effective assault on the shoulds is to say to your-self, "Now wait a minute. It's not a matter of should or shouldn't. My wife just left me and it really hurts. I don't like it one little bit!" By doing so, you are honestly stating how you feel and have become more accepting of your-self as being in pain. (Ideas in this section draw on the work of Dr. David Burns 1980.)

Tools to Build Coping Skills and Self-Confidence

Self-confidence is basically the ability to trust in your coping resources. Remember that when self-confidence begins to sink, you may forget that you functioned successfully in the past. You may tend to focus on your failures. Instead, you might think, "I need to remember that I'm strong and have handled problems in the past. I need to believe in myself. It'll be hard at first but I can do it."

The trick is not to try to fool yourself into believing that there are no risks or pain, or that you are completely without fault. Your goal is to acknowledge, accept, and gain perspective. Be more self-accepting, not self-critical. Recognize that your *thoughts* are contributing to your anxiety or depression. You're hurting yourself and you need to stop the negative thoughts. Actively replace your thoughts with positive coping statements (see list on page 92 for some samples which may fit you). Your self-confidence will begin to return.

Begin to challenge your thinking frequently. As soon as you notice an unpleasant feeling, reel it in; take a moment, write down your thoughts along with a more realistic response. (Jotting these thoughts down on paper is an especially effective way to become clear about how you are thinking, and to then gain a realistic perspective.) If you cannot do it on the spot, do it later in the day, taking a few minutes to go back over the events of the day and your thoughts. It takes a bit of time and effort to write things down, but the effects will be better if you bring your thoughts to awareness.

The strategies we've mentioned in this chapter actively interfere with negative thinking and can be helpful in restoring you self-confidence to deal with the demands of life. These techniques are not magical solutions, they are straightforward actions you can take *now* and can practice between sessions of brief therapy. Don't let their apparent simplicity fool you. These cognitive coping skills have been shown to be some of the most rapid and effective approaches to helping people regain control over unpleasant feelings. As you begin to feel better, you can develop effective decision-making and problem-solving skills that will help you gain an even greater sense of self-mastery.

In the next chapter we'll focus on taking direct action to change stressful events that arise in important interpersonal relationships.

Positive Self-Statements to Help You Cope

1. This feeling isn't comfortable or pleasant, but in this moment I can accept it.

2. I can be in pain, sad, anxious . . . and still deal with this situation.

3. I can handle it.

4. This is not an emergency. It's okay to think slowly about what's happening and how I feel.

5. This is not the worst thing that could happen.

6. This will pass.

7. I don't have to let this get to me; I'll ride through it.

8. I deserve to feel okay.

9. I don't have to do it right the first time; I'm not perfect and neither is anybody else.

10. I'm having a feeling that I don't like; it won't kill me, it just doesn't feel good.

11. These are just thoughts; I can change them.

12. I don't have to have all the answers; nobody else does either, though some folks think they do.

13. I have the right to change my mind about what I think about any given situation.

14. I have the right to make mistakes.

15. I have the right to feel anger.

16. I have the right to say "I don't know."

17. "I think I can, I think I can . . . "

Chapter 13

Getting Along with Others

Broken promises, unfair treatment, insensitivity, attempts to control, manipulate or dominate, unwillingness or inability to compromise, emotional, physical, or sexual abuse, harassment, dishonesty, guilt trips . . .

Relationships! "Can't live with 'em, can't live without 'em." Whether it's relatives, friends, lovers, or colleagues, the one thing you can count on is that relationships are not only a vital part of your existence, but one of life's biggest challenges.

And the differences! Values, style, needs, opinion, history, life circumstances, dispositions, temperament . . . people are definitely not all the same! Under the best of circumstances our differences add excitement and stimulation, but they inevitably also contribute to frustration and upset. Problems must be seen as an inevitable part of living.

Bells, Whistles, and Other Alarms

If you have experienced conflicts with others, you may recall some of your unpleasant feelings about your experience. Those feelings and your reactions to them have become a part of your own unique "early warning system" or alarm, alerting you to possible danger: "Something is wrong here."

One thing that's true about alarm systems is that they are most useful when you learn to work with them. You don't want to suffer too many false alarms, but when the alarm does go off, it's time to take action to prevent a difficult situation from becoming worse. The greater you understand and practice with the alarm the more helpful it can potentially be.

Psychologists have come to understand a number of fairly common alarms—reactions that are important cues for us to pay attention to so we know it's time to work at resolving conflict in our relationship. Here are a few examples:

- *Pent-up feelings.* Have a hard time being as direct and forthright as you would like? For a variety of reasons you may grit you teeth and keep your feelings to yourself. This "emotional constipation" can become quite limiting and uncomfortable, not only for you, but for others in your life.

- *Avoiding.* "If I don't confront it, if I put it off, maybe it will go away." Kind of like the ostrich who buries its head in the sand to avoid the stampede. Pretending "it's not there" may offer psychological respite in the moment—like the ostrich, you might luck out and not get run over—but in the middle of a stampede the odds aren't good. While fantasy and magical thinking can be fun and may provide the opportunity to practice in your mind's eye, they are rarely helpful in the long run.

- *Excuses, apologies, or justification.* There may be a time to provide a short, simple, direct explanation of why you decided to do or not do something. However, if this occurs more often than not, or if you often feel guilty and overly apologetic, it may be time for a change.

- *Putting yourself last.* Unless you're in the league of Buddha, Gandhi, or Jesus, putting yourself last works only occasionally. Every healthy relationship you find yourself in requires some degree of mutual give-and-take. It's not healthy to always put your own needs last or constantly give in to others at your own expense. We're not suggesting that you adopt the opposite extreme, always putting yourself first, but we want you to recognize that the "middle ground," involving mutual support and acceptance, will generally result in stronger, more vital relationships.

- *Putting yourself down.* Do you ever hear yourself or someone you know say something like, "This may sound stupid but . . . ," or "I'm sorry to disagree, but . . . "? When you think, feel or express negative beliefs about yourself, you not only put yourself down, you increase the likelihood of staying stuck, and minimize your options and possibilities for change. If you believe only the worst about yourself, it's time to develop a more reasonable, balanced perspective.

- *Aggressive or hostile behavior.* Do you find yourself exploding inside or outwardly toward others? Would people describe you as hostile and aggressive? It's normal and natural to feel angry and upset at various points in life, but to feel it all of the time or to take it out on yourself or others can be destructive.

  Aggression is a style of expressing feelings that rarely takes others' feelings into consideration. Some folks learned this style while growing up, and may believe it is the only way they can feel powerful or in control of a situation or relationship. While there are many circumstances that need to be dealt with directly—including expressing such negative feelings as anger or upset—it is rarely, if ever, more effective to express feelings aggressively rather than assertively.

  If you tend to be aggressive, your intimate relationships, if you're lucky enough to still have any, suffer. While you may attempt to deny it, this can result in a vicious circle of isolation and upset in which your aggressive feelings drive others away, resulting in you feeling even more angry and potentially aggressive.

- *Passive self-denial.* This style of dealing with others is also described as "timid" or "passive." While it is not normal to have strong feelings about *everything* in your life, it is not normal to pretend you don't have strong feelings about *anything.* This "whatever . . . ," shrug-the-shoulders style is typical of those who are afraid to be honest with themselves or others about how they feel. If this is true of you, it may be your secret hope that if you avoid being assertive you can minimize the discomfort you associate with conflict. You may have learned to live with more unhappiness in your life than necessary. The long-term cost of self-denial is enormously high, including increased vulnerability to possibly aggressive and abusive relationships.

Now that we've examined some unhealthy ways to deal with others, let's move on to a more reasonable, adaptive way of getting along, by expressing your feelings in a direct, appropriately assertive way.

Healthy Assertive Coping

If you find your relationships less than satisfying, disappointing, or painful, it may be that you've been following one or more of the unhealthy paths we've just discussed. If you want to be happier and feel more in control of your life, most therapists will recommend that you learn to become more assertive. That may sound a little scary at first, but please read on. We think you'll want to try it. *Assertiveness* is a word most of us have heard but may not really understand. Common usage often gives the mistaken idea that being assertive is the same as being aggressive. Both styles do involve expressing important feelings without holding back, but assertiveness tempers honesty with genuine concern, sensitivity, and respect for the other person's feelings. Assertiveness is a

Being assertive means being able to choose how you will act in any given relationship situation.

style of expression that is equally comfortable with both negative and positive feelings.

You've seen people who appear totally comfortable in
social situations, but the fact is that nobody's *born* assertive.
Assertion is a learned style that involves developing healthy
attitudes, overcoming some obstacles (such as anxiety), and
learning a few effective behavioral skills. Being assertive
means being able to *choose* how you will act in any given relationship situation.

It takes lots of practice to feel comfortable and natural
when being assertive. Even if you're shy, even if you're not as
confident as you would like, it's possible to learn to be assertive. Those who have developed the skill generally report
more satisfying relationships and increased self-confidence.

Getting Started

The most important thing to remember about assertiveness is that it's a matter of choice. You don't need to try to be
assertive all the time. The first step is to look at a particular
problem and honestly ask yourself, "Is this important enough
to justify action?" There are lots of times when it's honestly no
big deal—a passive stance may be fine. However, we want to
caution you about something: Everyone encounters situations
that in fact are very important, but some folks tell themselves,
"It's no big deal," even when it really matters. So it's essential
that you look at situations honestly and realistically, and prepare yourself to take assertive action when it counts.

Goals of Assertive Conflict Resolution

One goal of acting assertively, of course, is to bring about
a *change in a situation or in another person's behavior*. For example, if somebody is taking advantage of you, your goal might
be, "I want him to stop doing this."

A second important goal is to *increase your own self-
respect*. We want to strongly emphasize that the second goal—
increasing your own self-respect—really is the major goal in

being assertive. Before you go talk with somebody about an important issue, it's helpful to remind yourself of these two goals and to tell yourself, "Obviously I want to make a change in the situation; I'm going in there to request a change. Regardless of what happens, I'm going to take this opportunity to express how I feel and what my opinions are. Even if I don't get what I want, I'm going to state my feelings and opinions firmly, and then I'm going to be able to walk out of there with my head held high."

Consider the Risks

"What are the risks of being assertive?" Consider that question very consciously. If you are like a lot of people, you may imagine all sorts of dangerous or upsetting consequences of acting assertively. These assumptions about "what's going to happen" actually may govern whether or not you act assertively. Sometimes unpleasant things do happen. What these risks may be need to be examined closely, honestly, and realistically.

Let's take a look at a few:

- *"The other person might become upset, or angry, or hurt, or rejected."* Many people put off dealing with and confronting problem situations in relationships because they are afraid the other person is going to become extremely upset. The reality is that by avoiding the situation, you may perpetuate serious interpersonal problems for months or even for years, which could take a tremendous emotional toll on both of you. People tend to greatly overestimate the amount of emotional upset that actually may result when they confront another person. By and large, if you approach the other person, treating her with respect, showing some sensitivity to her feelings, and just being honest with her—without belittling her or putting her down—any upset that does occur will be very short-term. Deciding to confront the issue and deal with a temporary upset may be the first step toward permanent resolution.

- *"The other person may find a way to get back at me or to get even."* We want to caution you that being assertive is no guarantee that the other person is going to respond in a positive way. It would be great if every time you were assertive, the other person said, "Oh, that's fine. I understand." Sometimes that happens. Sometimes people are somewhat irate or upset, but these feelings pass, they're temporary. And in some situations being assertive with certain kinds of people can lead to some very serious problems. This is often the case if you are dealing with an emotionally unstable or immature person. A good example of this might be confronting a supervisor or boss who tends to be emotionally immature and who may, in fact, not like having an employee who is simply honest, direct, and mature. Some insecure people enjoy and gain satisfaction from dominating and controlling other people; their focus is making sure that people under them are submissive and not assertive. With a person like this, you run the risk of getting seriously hurt, in physical and non-physical ways, that can be very damaging. (Losing your job comes to mind.) You have to use your head about this possibility by asking yourself, "What do I know about this person? Based on my experience, do I feel that this person is mature enough to endure and to handle an honest confrontation?" Sometimes the answer is "No, he's not." In that case, it may pay to choose to be non-assertive.

- *"The assertion may fail."* You may stick your neck out, you may ask for something, you may confront someone, and she may say, "Forget it! No way!" Many people are very afraid to look foolish, or to feel helpless, or not to know what to do should the assertion fail. One response you may wish to consider in such a situation is to respond quickly, "I'm sorry you feel that way. This issue is very important to me, and I hope you'll give some thought to what I've said."

(Shortly, we will be giving you additional "backup plans" for these situations. When you have decided to

approach a problem situation in which there's even a slight
chance that the assertion might fail, having a pre-arranged
backup plan is important: "What am I going to do if the assertion doesn't work?"

Risk versus Reward: Short Run and Long Run

It's a natural tendency for people to focus on the immediate
emotional issues that might come up when they confront others and talk to them assertively. We think it's important for
you to ask yourself, "Okay, I need to consider this other person might feel sad or might feel irritated or might get angry
with me at the moment. But let me think about the long-term
consequences of these responses. What do I think really will
happen in the long run? Is she going to continue to be *very* sad
or *very* upset for a prolonged time if I confront her?" Consciously appreciating the view that negative responses may be
short-term, can make the decision to be assertive easier.

Considering the long-term positive consequences is also
helpful. What may be going on inside your head when you
think about being assertive are the short-term negative consequences. But we think it's very important as you're preparing
to assert yourself to ask, "Once I get through with this, even
though there may be some upset, I wonder what the *positive
results* could be?" These positive outcomes might be seen in
terms of both the situation and yourself. You might ask yourself, "I wonder if in the long run this decision to be assertive
will solve the problem? Maybe this problem is something we
won't have to deal with over and over and over again. Maybe
I'm not going to be walking around with this pent-up anger
and resentment all the time. It might make it easier for us to
get in and work on our relationship, to truly feel better about
things." Another positive consequence would be, "These people are going to know where I stand. Maybe they'll think twice
before they try to take advantage of me again. I'm not a person

who is willing to be pushed around; I'm going to stand up for myself."

Here's another positive result: "Even though this might be tough in some ways, just maybe after I've been assertive, I can walk out of here and tell myself, 'By gosh, you know what? I did that! I'm proud of myself!'"

Planning for Action

Systematically going over each of the steps mentioned above, in your own mind, can be helpful. It is a way to prepare yourself emotionally and to get to a place of feeling okay about your decision to speak out. In addition, especially if the situation is important to you or very emotional, it also may be helpful to write out exactly what you're going to say to the person ahead of time, practicing out loud several times, until you are expressing your thoughts in a way that feels right. If you have a trustworthy friend, you may wish to practice with him or her; let your friend pretend to be the other person as you rehearse what you are going to say, until you feel comfortable.

Practicing an assertive response, even two or three times, can make a big difference in feeling solid about how you're coming across. If no one is available to help you, practicing in front of a mirror can be helpful too, because it gives you an opportunity to watch and hear yourself and then to make some improvements. Then, when you are actually getting ready for the meeting, you already know how you're going to come across. (If you have the luxury of a video camera, that's an even better tool to help you practice and improve.)

Key Ingredients of Assertive Behavior

When Shawna decided to tell Tim about how she felt, she made a point to have his full attention. She started by stating, "This is very important to me, and I'd like you to listen to what I have to say." She also consciously made herself look directly into his eyes and began to talk in a firm, but non-hostile voice. "I think I have said the same words to him a hundred times, but this time he heard me. It wasn't what I said as much as how *I said it. He got the message that I meant business."*

As we consider what being assertive "looks like," and what the different aspects of assertion are, it's helpful to break assertive behavior down into three component parts:

- *Verbal content.* This refers to the particular words that you choose to speak, what you decide to say. There are two guidelines that you can use to make sure your verbal content is assertive; one is KISS, which stands for "Keep It Short and Simple." Many times when people are trying to be assertive, they get sidetracked, get off onto some long explanations, excuses, justification, apologies, and so forth. Getting to the point as quickly as possible will really pay off.

    The second point about content is something called "I Language." When you're expressing what you feel, it's an effective strategy to say, "This is how *I* feel." Lots of times people inadvertently will say, *"You make me* feel sad," *"You make me* feel unhappy," *"You make me* feel angry," and so forth. This approach can present some problems; when you say *"You make me* feel . . . ," in a sense, you're casting yourself in the role of a helpless person. And this role can increase feelings of anxiety and insecurity. There's something about saying "I feel sad" or "I feel angry" that helps the message come across as more powerful. What's more, you're maintaining more self-control. Saying, "Look, I feel this way," actually increases and enhances your self-esteem and self-respect. Also, if you say to another person, "You make me feel" a certain way, that tends to greatly increase defensiveness. If you want to talk with others and negotiate for change or confront them about their behavior, statements that increase defensiveness decrease the chances of success. People simply tend to be more responsive and open to hearing someone say, "I feel sad," "I feel angry," and so forth. Take responsibility for your own feelings by using I language.

- *Vocal tone.* An assertive vocal tone is firm and direct. You're not coming across in an overly loud voice, which might scare people or make them feel you're aggressive, or, by contrast, in a silent, meek, whinny kind of voice. A firm, solid, well-modulated tone of voice conveys "I mean what I'm saying."

- *Gestures, body language, and eye contact.* Probably the most important non-verbal element of communication is eye contact. When people are afraid, anxious, or non-assertive, it's tough to make eye contact. Just watch the next time someone's talking to you and feeling anxious. There's something powerful and convincing about looking someone in the eye and saying, "Hey, this is how I feel; this is my opinion." It's a non-verbal message that lets people know, "I mean what I'm saying."

Backup Plans

In the real world, there are times when your assertions don't work they way you hoped.

The other person may respond in ways designed to get you to back off. Let's say that you're confronting someone about an emotionally charged situation in which a lot of your feelings are being revealed. Some people will respond by saying, "You're just too emotional about this!" or "It's just like a woman to be so emotional!" One way to respond to this is to say, "You know what? I *do* have strong feelings about this issue, and I am going to make my point again."

"I know this is hard to hear . . . but this issue is important . . . We're going to work together and resolve this."

Then jump right back in and reassert yourself. Reasserting your point in spite of the other person's response is an effective way of stopping the other person from using this type of manipulation. You have not agreed that you are *too* emotional. You have simply affirmed your strong feelings.

The other person may respond to your assertion with tears and a lot of guilt messages. One way to deal with this is to say, "I know this is hard to hear, I know this is causing you pain, but this issue is important, and I want to repeat myself because we're going to work together and resolve this." Again, what you've done is to stop the other person's attempt to use guilt to get you to back off from your assertive response.

Some people may quibble with you about the legitimacy of what you feel. You have the right to state feelings and opinions without justifying them. One way to react to this response is to say, "Regardless of the reasons, this is my opinion," or "Well, let's face it, we may not agree on this, but all the same, this is how I feel." Again, reasserting yourself and not bowing to the demand for justifications.

When dealing with an extremely angry or aggressive person, it can be helpful to say, "I can see that you're very angry and upset, but it's important that we resolve this issue, and we are going to talk about this. If we can't talk about it now, that's okay. But I'm going to come back, and we're going to talk about it later."

Is It Time for Action in Your Real World?

We hope you'll find this discussion about assertion helpful. Deciding to confront truly difficult interpersonal problems and act in an assertive way is often hard to do and may be accompanied by a good deal of uneasiness, and sometimes actual risks. Many people have found it helpful to seek out an assertiveness training group—a type of group therapy that helps people learn how to act in an assertive way, provides opportunities for practice and role playing, and offers support. Many have benefited by reading the excellent self-help books on assertion that we have listed in the References section of this book. And working directly with your therapist can be valuable—particularly if you are prepared to resolve significant problems in important relationships. The therapist can provide guidance and support.

As you might guess, becoming assertive takes hard work and lots of practice. Many of us have to unlearn behavior we have practiced for years and learn new, healthier behavior and attitudes. Fortunately, assertiveness training has flourished and it's likely that you'll find workshops covered by your insurance benefit or sponsored by a number of organizations in your community.

Dealing with significant conflict with others can be incredibly difficult. That's a reality that has to be acknowledged. At the same time, the approaches advocated in this chapter have been in wide use during the past twenty-five years and have a solid track record. Being assertive is not a cure-all for resolving the emotionally charged conflicts in your life, but it certainly is an approach that has a good chance of success.

You have a right to say *no* to emotional abuse, to express your own feelings, and to ask for changes in another's behavior. We encourage you to learn to be assertive.

Chapter 14

Staying Healthy/ Reducing Stress

As you think about how brief therapy may help you deal with emotional distress, consider this: *Physical problems often cause emotional distress, and emotional upsets may produce physical symptoms.* In this chapter, we'll take a closer look at how you can reduce emotional stress by keeping yourself physically well and learning to relax.

Stressful life events often bring on unpleasant and sometimes painful or dangerous physical symptoms including tension headaches, insomnia, fatigue, restlessness, loss of sex drive, ulcers, high blood pressure, and decreased energy. Recent evidence suggests that prolonged, significant emotional distress can also impair the function of the immune system, increasing our risk of certain infectious diseases, and retarding recovery from physical illnesses.

Three primary approaches have been shown to be quite effective in reducing some of the physical symptoms associated with life stress: *changing unhealthy habits, relaxation, and appropriate use of medications.*

Change Unhealthy Habits

Research has shown over and over again that under the impact of emotional distress, people develop bad habits, including excessive use of alcohol, tobacco, caffeine, and junk foods. These poor nutritional and health habits can, in the long run, result in serious physical illnesses, such as cardiac disease and cancer. There are a host of short-term risks as well.

Alcohol: Arguably the most used—and abused—drug in the United States, alcohol can provide a very potent and quick sense of release from physical tension and can promote a temporary feeling of euphoria or relaxation. Many people who are experiencing emotional pain seek the quick relief alcohol provides. While we don't intend to be moralistic about the issues of alcohol use, evidence clearly shows that the use of alcohol can backfire, especially over a prolonged period of time, on a regular basis, and in moderate-to-high amounts.

Alcohol, in and of itself, is responsible for tremendous aggravation of the symptoms of depression and anxiety. However, it is a seductive substance, because the immediate result of drinking is relief; the person perceives that the alcohol is helpful. But prolonged use actually results in a change in the neurochemistry of the brain, increasing—not relieving—anxiety and depression. Avoiding, reducing, or eliminating alcohol intake during stressful times is one key self-care action that you can take. *(Note: If you have been drinking heavily, it is important to know that abrupt discontinuation of alcohol can result in very unpleasant and sometimes dangerous withdrawal symptoms. Under these circumstances alcohol detox should only be done under medical supervision.)*

Caffeine: This widely used drug is found in some unexpected places: in coffee, of course, and in a host of other substances that people consume, including tea, certain other drinks (especially colas), and—unfortunately!—chocolate. It can also be found in pain medications (Excedrin) and diet pills. Like alcohol, caffeine is a seductive drug. One common physical effect of stress is a sense of fatigue and decreased energy. Caffeine is a potent stimulant and can provide, rather quickly, a sense of improved alertness and energy. Some researchers believe that caffeine has mild but transient antidepressant effects and may be used by some chronically depressed people to elevate their moods.

Caffeine can also backfire. Studies of caffeine use and abuse indicate that when people ingest more than 250 milligrams per day of caffeine, there is a significant likelihood of developing such stress-related symptoms as jitteriness, tension, anxiety, and insomnia. The risks of symptoms increase dramatically when the amount of caffeine surpasses 500 milligrams per day. (The average cup of coffee contains approximately 150 milligrams of caffeine, and the typical cola drink or tea contains around 50 milligrams of caffeine.)

Another often unrecognized but important symptom of caffeine use is disruption of the quality of sleep. Even if you're able to go to sleep, large amounts of caffeine may produce restless sleep. As a result, you'll fail to get adequate rest during the night, which leads to excessive daytime fatigue. To combat this fatigue, the typical coffee/cola drinker chooses—you guessed it—to drink more caffeine.

In difficult times, it may seem silly to worry about the amount of coffee you're drinking. Many people "pooh-pooh" the notion that caffeine contributes to emotional problems, but clinical research shows that caffeine can cause or exacerbate stress-related symptoms.

The bottom line here: *One decisive action you can take during times of stress is to reduce or eliminate caffeine.* Note that if you are accustomed to drinking large amounts of caffeine, and you quit "cold turkey," you will likely experience significant caffeine withdrawal symptoms: anxiety, restlessness, tension, and headaches. Thus, if you have become accustomed to ingesting large amounts of caffeine, you'll want to *gradually* decrease your intake of caffeine over a period of two to three weeks, progressively replacing caffeinated beverages with decaffeinated beverages.

Exercise: At times of great emotional distress, you may experience a tremendous sense of decreased energy and fatigue. And during such times, motivating yourself to engage in normal physical exercise becomes even more difficult. You'll probably feel like stopping your normal exercise program, perhaps reducing your normal daily activity level as well. Don't do it. Fatigue feeds on itself. The more tired you feel, the more you're inclined to sit on the couch or lie in bed. Reduced activity almost always leads to a progressive cycle of increasing fatigue.

Another common outcome of emotional distress is significant weight gain because of decreased activity and an increased appetite for inappropriate foods. Weight gain can have negative consequences for both physical functioning and emotional well-being. Significant weight gain may lead to feelings of inadequacy, low self-esteem, obesity, hypertension, and diabetes.

An important decision you can make during difficult times of emotional distress is to take care of yourself as best you can, focusing on proper nutrition, exercise, and a reduction or avoidance of alcohol or caffeine. These are not magical solutions—no one has ever survived emotionally traumatic times simply by ceasing to drink coffee. But such actions can be simple ways to take control of part of your life, to reduce some amount of stress-related symptoms, and to promote a sense of physical well-being.

Learn to Relax

In the early days of psychosomatic medicine, it was commonplace for patients to complain to their family physicians about noticeable physical symptoms, only to be told, "It's just stress" or "It's all in your mind." As a result, many people left the doctor feeling they were crazy, misunderstood, or just imagining these problems.

Emotional distress is more than just a state of mind; it's much more than just feeling bad or having negative, unpleasant thoughts. During times of emotional stress, bona fide physical changes and symptoms do occur, some of which are uncomfortable and painful and some of which can actually lead to life-threatening illnesses. There is clear evidence to suggest that significant stress, including anxiety and depression, can lead to profound changes in brain chemistry, including the release of many different hormones from the endocrine glands of the body (the pituitary gland, the adrenal gland, and the thyroid gland).

Hormones are specifically designed to regulate normal metabolic functioning, controlling or influencing many basic biological rhythms, drives, and processes. Without the combined effort of intricately complex hormone systems, survival would be impossible. However, during times of stress the brain can activate the endocrine system in a way that results in such stress-related physical symptoms as rapid heart rate, high blood pressure, and decrease or increase of metabolic activity. In addition, the hormone system can profoundly affect the functioning of the immune system, altering the functioning of specific white blood cells.

The ultimate solution to reducing stress is to come to terms with painful life events or to alter the course of those events in your life. In the short run, you can employ a number of strategies to reduce physical distress. Relaxation exercises (sometimes accompanied by biofeedback) and meditation techniques are widely used as a treatment (or adjunct treatment) for many physical illnesses, including migraine headaches, hypertension, ulcers, chronic pain conditions, chronic fatigue, and others.

When friends are under stress it is common advice to tell them to "Just relax." We're not talking about "just relaxing" here, but offering specific procedures that have been demonstrated to have a profound effect on physical functioning.

The ultimate solution to reducing stress is to come to terms with painful life events . . .

The techniques described on pages 112–115 are two proven procedures for learning to relax deeply.

You'll have to discover for yourself whether the *progressive muscle relaxation* technique or *visualization* (or a combination of the two) works best. Please keep in mind that simple relaxation techniques alone don't solve major life crises. "Just relaxing" or "taking it easy" are not the answers as we go through difficult times. We also want to emphasize that the specific procedures described here are of proven value—hundreds of careful studies have shown their effectiveness. Sitting in front of the TV with a beer—or even vacationing in Hawaii—may sound easier and perhaps more appealing, but those activities are not particularly helpful in countering stress over the long haul.

Relaxation Techniques

The following techniques have been found to be helpful ways to learn to relax completely: progressive muscle relaxation and visualization.

Progressive Muscle Relaxation

During times of stress, particular muscles and muscle groups tend automatically to become tense. Progressive muscle relaxation techniques are designed to reduced tension in most of the body's major muscle groups.

The relaxation procedure requires a period of time when you will not be disturbed. Sit in a comfortable chair, or recline on a couch or on a carpeted floor. Close your eyes and take two slow, deep breaths. As you exhale slowly, notice the gradual release of tension in chest and shoulder muscles. Feel the weight of your body against the chair (couch, floor), and the gentle pull of gravity as you settle into the chair. After a few moments, you can begin a series of simple exercises, tensing particular muscles, holding the tension for a count of "three" and then releasing. Each time you tense and then release, you can enhance the effect by paying special attention to the experience of relaxation/letting go that occurs immediately after release.

Allow ten or fifteen seconds between each tensing of muscles before proceeding to the next muscle group. The tensing exercises begin with the feet and progress like this:

1. Feet/toes

2. Calves/lower legs

3. Thighs

4. Buttocks (squeeze together)

5. Abdomen

6. Lower back (arch)

7. Chest (hold in a deep breath)

8. Hands (make fists)

9. Upper arms

10. Shoulders (shrug)

11. Face (squeeze eyes and mouth closed)

12. Face (open eyes and mouth)

Many experts on relaxation techniques recommend fifteen to twenty minutes twice a day to go through this exercise, especially when you're first learning the procedure. It's been our experience, however, that few people will find time to do this on a regular basis. A realistic alternative, after you've practiced for a week or so and learned how to relax deeply, is to abbreviate the technique by omitting the tensing step and simply relaxing each muscle group in turn. This whole procedure can easily be done in two to three minutes, and repeated several times a day. When time allows, you can, of course, give yourself permission to expand the procedure and achieve an ever deeper sense of relaxation.

You'll notice immediately a significant reduction of muscular tension. More important, if the exercise is done several times a day (even briefly) on a regular basis, it can reduce chronic tension levels. You may notice less daytime fatigue, more productive energy, and an improved ability to fall asleep, due in large part to a decreased release of stress hormones.

Visualization

Many different visualization techniques have been developed. Here's a description of one of the most commonly employed:

Begin by finding a quiet time and comfortable chair or couch. Close your eyes and take two slow, deep breaths. Notice the physical sensations of relaxation as you gently exhale.

After a few moments, imagine yourself standing at the top of a flight of stairs with ten steps. In a moment you can begin to see yourself slowly and gradually walking down the stairs, one at a time. When you begin your descent, you will notice a sense of increasing relaxation as you move downward. With each step, experience the feeling of deeper and deeper relaxation. As you take each step, silently count to yourself: ten . . . nine . . . eight . . . lower and lower as you go. Throughout your descent, you feel safe and in control, as you choose to let go of tension. The mental image of downward movement has been found to trigger a relaxation response.

As you reach the bottom of the stairs . . . two . . . one . . . let your mind take you to a particular setting, a place you know that you associate with feelings of comfort, security, and well-being. It may be a beautiful meadow, a warm, sunny beach, or a rustic cabin in the forest. The choice is yours as you create your own personal image of serenity. The experience of relaxation is enhanced by taking particular note of all sensory experiences in your image (the sights, sounds, smells, and feelings of the peaceful setting).

After a few minutes, you can decide to leave the relaxing setting by slowly counting from three to one . . . three . . .

two . . . one . . . as your eyes open and you again are fully alert, but relaxed.

Progressive muscle relaxation and visualization clearly do reduce physical tension, and they are ways that you can give yourself some amount of self-nurturing. They are direct ways to exert some control of tension while taking other actions to promote coping and emotional healing. (For a more complete discussion, please see Davis et al. 1995; Benson 1975.)

Your therapist can assist you with these procedures, if you need additional help, or they may have other suggestions to add to your repertoire of tools for dealing with physical and emotional stress. You can't have too many!

Chapter 15

Acute Distress Tolerance Skills

Regardless of the circumstance or specific stress symptoms, many people, at times, encounter very intense or overwhelming distress (anger, frustration, irritation, anxiety, tremendous uneasiness, or sadness). At such times there is obviously no 100 percent quick fix to eliminate distress. However, the following approaches have been shown to be very successful in helping people to quickly turn down the volume on intense distress. Not only can these approaches decrease emotional suffering, but when people get in the habit of using these, it can lead to a greater sense of emotional self-control.

Sixty-Second Reality Check

Especially during times of stress it's common to experience moments of strong, upsetting feelings. One form of "homework" that just takes a minute is what we call the *sixty-second reality check*. This is a simple but powerful technique that can often help you gain perspective and reduce distress in just a minute. Here's how it works: As soon as something has happened that has triggered a strong feeling, take just a moment to go through the following list:

1. Does this (what's just happened) really matter to me?
2. In the grand scheme of things, how big a deal is it?

    Is it a true catastrophe?

    Is it likely to seem like a big deal in twenty-four hours?

    Is it likely to seem like a big deal in one week?
3. Am I taking it personally?
4. If I react now will it:

    Probably be helpful?

    Probably make things worse?
5. Would it make sense to take time to think through the situation and then decide how to react?
6. Are my thoughts and actions helping me or hurting me?

    What I'm thinking or telling myself right now—is it helpful or is it hurtful?

It is important to emphasize that this technique is *not* designed to help you talk yourself out of feeling the way you do. It's very important to be true to how you really feel. At the same time, reflect a bit on how you really see a situation, so that you may then choose wisely how you want to respond. This brief "reality check" is a good way to gain perspective quickly and avoid impulsive reactions.

Turning Down the Volume on Strong Feelings

Once again the intention here is *not* to deny or minimize real, honest feelings, but rather to do something that can help you feel in *control* of your emotions. People often say or think certain words and phrases that operate like emotion amplifiers. Often, simply rephrasing (or reframing) your thoughts and words de-intensifies emotions without negating how you truly feel. Here is a very brief list of rephrases that you may find helpful.

You Say or Think	Rephrased
I really need it!	It's not that I absolutely need it ... rather, I really want it
I feel guilty and am a bad person	I am not a bad person, but I do feel regret
It shouldn't be that way	It is and I don't like it
I'm being too sensitive	I do have strong feelings about this
It's a catastrophe	It's important and it matters a lot ... although it may not be a complete catastrophe

Quickly Reducing Physical Aspects of Intense Emotions

The following have been shown to be effective ways to reduce some aspects of overwhelming emotions. Please keep in mind that these approaches are not designed to completely block out feelings. As we've stated before, most times people need to be aware of inner emotions. However, the following five techniques can help you reduce emotional intensity. Don't be fooled by the apparent simplicity of these approaches!

Exercise

Very vigorous exercise for a period of ten to twenty minutes is considered to result in increases of the neuro-chemical serotonin in the brain. Increases in serotonin levels are often accompanied by noticeable and rapid decreases in emotional distress (especially anger and irritability). The benefits are short term (lasting for twenty to thirty minutes generally), but the decrease in physical arousal often greatly facilitates one's ability to think more clearly, regain perspective, and counter the tendency to react in impulsive or maladaptive ways.

Crying

A perfectly natural and normal response to stress (not just sadness, but also frustration and anger) is to cry. Despite our society's prohibition on crying (especially for men: "Don't be a crybaby" ... "Don't cry over spilt milk" ...), scientific evidence exists to suggest that a "good cry" can dramatically reduce stress. Dr. William Frey (1983) has found that emotional tears contain stress hormones that are secreted and eliminated from the body. Additionally, the majority of people studied report a significant decrease in arousal and a sense of relief after crying (85% for women and 73% for men in these studies). The key is to give yourself permission to cry, without guilt or self-criticism. The research on the biology of crying reveals this to be a remarkable, built-in mechanism for rapid tension reduction and emotional self-soothing.

Dietary Solutions

A highly complex carbohydrate snack (without protein) is felt to increase absorption of essential amino acids into the brain, and may result in a degree of emotional calming (which can begin to be felt quickly and may last for one to one and a half hours). Except when excessive weight gain is a problem, this is a viable approach for some people.

Muscle Relaxation

Most states of intense distress involve considerable physical arousal and increased muscular tension. Relaxation techniques may be difficult to use in the throes of intense distress; however, soaking in a hot bath can often rapidly reduce some of the physical arousal.

Eye-Movement Techniques

In the 1990s it was discovered that back-and-forth eye movements can often rapidly produce a calming effect. This technique involves a set of twenty to thirty, back-and-forth eye movements. The person can, while holding the head still, gaze from side to side (shifting right and then left at the rate of about once a second). Initially, this is best done with the eyes open, but can eventually be done with your eyes closed. Exactly how this works to reduce distress is not well understood. Some research has suggested that it blocks anxious thoughts, while other research has demonstrated that it can lead to metabolic changes in the brain (as demonstrated in studies using PET: a sophisticated technique for observing brain activity). Generally the twenty to thirty back-and-forth eye movements are repeated three or four times, with a few minutes between each series of movements when the person relaxes.

All of these approaches can be taught and practiced in therapy sessions, and then used between sessions during times of increased distress. At the heart of such techniques is acquiring effective coping skills and the restoration of a sense of emotional control.

Chapter 16

Doing "Homework" That Heals

THERE ARE SEVERAL easy things you can do between sessions that can help speed up the process of therapy. It's "homework"—but you won't be graded. These simple strategies have been developed, tested, and found to be quite helpful for people going through a wide array of difficult times. Let's take a look at six specific "homework" strategies.

What Works and What Doesn't

Often during times of stress, people conclude, "Nothing I do seems to help." Most times this statement is only partially true.

Jim and Mary come to a brief therapy session and continue to talk about marital problems. They just told the therapist that "We had a bad week." The therapist listened to the details, and at some point asked, "Were there any good times during the past week?" The couple said, "Yes . . . Saturday was pretty good."

You can look at this kind of situation and simply think, "Well, it was nice to have at least one good day" . . . and then, just forget about it. An alternative, however, is to think, "*Why* was it a good day? Could I have *two* good days next week?"

The therapist encouraged Jim and Mary to think carefully about Saturday, and try to discover any clues as to why things went well. Mary said, "Saturday, Jim saw that I was over-whelmed with the kids and he came up to me and said, 'Let me help out' . . . That was kinda unique for him to say some-thing like this, and I think it set the tone for the whole day. I really appreciated it."

When Jim confirmed the story, the therapist said, "I have a suggestion. We've focused a lot on problems and what doesn't work. But you've just told me that there really are times when the two of you can have a good day. I think it would be helpful to start paying attention to the good times. When you feel good about each other or you feel close, sit down and think, 'What made this possible? . . . What did I say or do, what did she say or do that really made a difference?' And write it down in a notebook. I know there are some seri-ous problems in your relationship, but there may be some solutions there too. Your homework assignment is to start not-ing those more positive times and start keeping a notebook—jotting down things that help and things that work. I think it'll help. Are you willing to give it a try?"

Many people discover to their surprise that there are some things they already do that succeed in reducing distress or minimizing conflicts. These are strengths you can build on!

Psychiatrist Gordon Deckert also suggests a simple and straightforward idea. When you keep trying to deal with a recurring problem in a particular way, and it doesn't work, stop and take a close look at what you're doing (that doesn't work) and at the very least, just don't do *that*! Most of us are creatures of habit and it's normal to do things in the "usual way"—even when the evidence is abundant that it doesn't work!

Mike gives us another example. Whenever he had a frus-trating week he'd feel depressed, discouraged, and hopeless. His usual solution was to shut himself away in his apartment all weekend . . . not going outside and not having contact with others. His therapist asked him if this "solution" was helpful.

Mike replied, "I don't feel like doing anything but hiding out at home all weekend, but I guess it doesn't help much . . . By Sunday night I usually feel worse."

His therapist inquired, "Have there ever been times when you were feeling down, but you *didn't* lock yourself away in your apartment?" Mike answered, "Yes . . . on occasion." He went on to elaborate about these rare occasions when he didn't *feel* like going out, but he forced himself to leave his apartment and go to the mall, or to the park, or bowling with a friend. And most times it helped him feel somewhat better.

The best way to approach this is to look carefully at what you do when times are difficult (maybe even write it down on paper) and then ask yourself, "Does this help me? Is it a good solution?" Some solutions aren't chosen; they feel automatic. And some solutions backfire; they either don't help or even make things feel worse. You do have choices. Take action! Even if you can't invent a great solution, at least stop doing things that don't work.

Positive Activity Diary

Annie is a thirty-five-year-old woman who came to brief therapy complaining of depression: "I can't get anything accomplished. I'm at home all day with the kids. By the time my husband gets home, the house is a wreck. I look at my house and think, 'What's wrong with me?' I don't even work. I'm just a housewife and I can't get anything done. I feel out of control of my whole life!" She considered herself an inadequate mother and housekeeper, who "does nothing productive." Since Annie has three children, ages one, two, and four, it was hard for her therapist to believe her statements, "I don't even work," and "I can't get anything done."

The therapist asked Annie to start keeping an *activity diary*, at least for one day. He asked her to write down *everything* she did, even small things like picking up a toy or getting a drink for one of her children. She brought to the next session a small notebook with many pages filled. She said, "I can't believe it. As I was writing everything down, it hit me. I'm continuously busy from morning 'til night. In fact, it was hard to keep up with the writing . . . I know I missed some things. Maybe my house looks like a wreck, but at least I know that I'm working my butt off. I *am* getting a lot done each day."

Especially if you feel overwhelmed or depressed, it's easy to overlook or minimize your accomplishments. At the end of the day you may conclude, "The day was wasted. I got nothing done." This perception lowers self-esteem and brings on a sense of defeat. An activity diary can help present a realistic view of events.

There are two ways you can do this. First, *write down every single activity*, as Annie did. This does take some time and is not practical for most of us on a regular basis. Still, doing it for a day or two can be helpful, as it was for Annie. A practical approach for use on a daily basis is to *record the major events* of each day: *tasks completed* (or progress made toward completion); *positive events* (receiving a compliment, pampering yourself with a hot bubble bath, having a nice lunch with a friend, getting a letter, feeling good about a job well done); and *experiences* that matter to you (spending time with your child, gardening, writing a letter to a friend, saying a prayer).

This process works best if you keep it simple and easy. It is best to jot down only brief three-to-five-word statements. Then, review the list at the end of the day. Even very distressed people who feel as though they accomplished absolutely nothing in a day are often surprised to find out that in fact they've done many things and experience some moments of pleasure. This approach is easy to put into action and can give immediate payoffs. It's an important way to avoid feelings of helplessness and low self-esteem.

Mood-Rating Chart

People who are under tremendous stress commonly look back over a period of time and remember primarily the negative feelings and events. They tend to conclude, "I've had an awful week. Everything went wrong, the whole week was terrible." This type of memory (which accentuates unpleasant experiences) can actually make stress worse. Believing that nothing positive happens in your life, or that you are always extremely depressed, can result in increased feelings of despair and pessimism. The fact is that *even very stressed people are not 100 percent distressed all of the time.* Even during very hard times people experience ups and downs. A person's mood is almost never completely stable. It is important and helpful to have an accurate and realistic perception of your moods and to be able to monitor changes in mood over time. An effective way to accomplish this is to use a *daily mood rating chart.* A number of studies have demonstrated that simply tracking and rating your moods on a daily basis has the effect of decreasing stress. At first glance this might seem absurd but let's look at this approach and understand how keeping track can help.

The use of a mood rating chart is simple. Take a look at the sample chart, page 128. (Feel free to make copies of this chart for your personal use.) Place a copy of the chart on your bedside table, and each night take a few moments to review the day. Ask yourself: "Overall, how did I feel today?" and then rate your feelings on a scale of plus 7 (extremely happy day) to minus 7 (extremely unhappy day). Most people will notice that there is a good deal of change in mood from day to day.

Daniel is a forty-two-year-old college professor who has been experiencing painful depressive symptoms since his wife asked him for a divorce a month ago. During his first therapy session he said, "Every single day, I feel paralyzed with depression. I have no energy, no motivation, and no happiness." During the next week he completed a daily mood rating chart and brought it in to the next session (please see page 129). In looking at this chart, he commented, "There were several days when I felt extremely depressed, but now looking back over the week, there were a couple of days that were not terrible, and most of the time I was not at rock bottom." This

Daily Mood Rating Chart

Starting Date: _____

Days:	1	2	3	4	5	6	7	8	9	10	11	12	13	14	15	16	17	18	19	20	21	22	23	24	25	26	27	28
+7																												
+6																												
+5																												
+4																												
+3																												
+2																												
+1																												
0																												
-1																												
-2																												
-3																												
-4																												
-5																												
-6																												
-7																												

Mood Rating:

+7 Best day of my life　　　0 Neutral　　　-7 Absolutely worst day of my life

Daily Mood Rating Chart   Daniel

Days:		1	2	3	4	5	6	7

Mood Rating chart with vertical axis labeled "Mood Rating:" from +7 down to -7. Plotted points (X): Day 1 at -2, Day 2 at -5, Day 3 at -5, Day 4 at -2, Day 5 at 0, Day 6 at -1, Day 7 at -2.

chart was helpful for him in two ways. First, it helped him remember more accurately and realistically how he was feeling. He soon realized that his depression, while certainly a painful experience, was not 100 percent pervasive. This acknowledgment helped to inspire hope, and left him feeling not quite so powerless. Second, he was able to use the chart over a period of two months to monitor his recovery from depression. After eight weeks of therapy, he said, "I've been noticing that gradually, over the past weeks, more and more of my days are good days. I still get discouraged and have some crummy days, but there definitely is a positive trend. I am feeling better."

Keeping Perspective

Another homework project you may find helpful is to make a list of "things that matter." In the midst of hard times, it's easy to focus mainly on bad stuff, and to lose sign of positive aspects of life. Our college professor, Daniel, made the following list:

Things That Matter to Me

1. My relationship with my kids
2. My teaching job and how I have an impact on my students
3. My involvement in church and our fund-raising activities
4. Reading exciting novels
5. Listening to rock and roll music
6. Sailing
7. Exercising at the YMCA
8. Talking to my sister on the phone
9. Writing or calling old friends
10. Driving in the country on a sunny weekend afternoon
11. The fact that I am a decent person and a good father
12. My sense of humor

Daniel wrote this list on a piece of paper, taped it to his bathroom mirror, and on the bottom in red ink wrote: "Dan— Don't forget these things. They are important!" His divorce was tough and many days were filled with sadness. But keeping in touch with positive things about himself and remembering to notice those things that matter helped him take it through even really hard days.

The homework activities in this chapter (and others that your therapist may suggest) can be of particular value if you review them with your therapist throughout the course of your brief therapy. The ideas are flexible. Work with your therapist to adapt them to your needs so they will contribute most to your emotional healing.

Chapter 17

Strengthening Your "Self"

Citizens in coastal regions of the Southeastern United States occasionally must prepare for the onslaught of a hurricane. With a day or two of warning, people in their communities place boards on windows, tie down trees, and secure other possessions, bracing for the storm. No amount of human action can lessen the force of the hurricane winds, but the preparation can make a significant difference in how well people weather the storm.

Similarly, during times of emotional crisis people can take steps to ride out emotional storms more successfully. These actions, we believe, have one thing in common: They strengthen a person's *sense of self*.

But what exactly is this notion of sense of self? Maybe it can best be described by giving examples of an underdeveloped sense of self and in contrast, a solidly developed sense of self. (See list on page 132.)

A childhood in which a person is truly loved, valued, and nurtured is the foundation for a solid sense of self. Yet many, many people did not have an idyllic childhood; for lots of us, growing up was difficult (sometimes extremely difficult). Fortunately, there are a number of things you can do to discover and strengthen your sense of self. Regardless of the emotional stresses you may be encountering, you can likely benefit from the suggestions that follow.

Underdeveloped Sense of Self

- You're easily manipulated by others.

- In the presence of powerful others, you lose sight of how you really feel and what you want. Readily changing your needs and opinions to please others.

- You're unclear about your own preferences and priorities.

- You often act out of compliance or an over-readiness to compromise or please others.

- You're unable to clearly define and pursue important life activities (job, hobbies, social causes).

- You are living your life for others, not out of your own unique, inner self.

- You easily lose your good mood if you encounter someone who is depressed or irritated.

A More Solidly Developed Sense of Self*

- You trust your own values, beliefs, and feelings.

- You believe you are the only person who really knows you.

- You're reasonably clear about how you really feel and what you truly want.

- You're able to maintain your relationships with others in difficult times.

- You're able to take positions on things that matter.

- You live by your own personal values, beliefs, and limits.

- You're able to acknowledge and benefit from your strengths and your weaknesses.

- You trust your intuition, hunches, and "gut feelings."

- You have compassion for yourself (without feeling guilty).

---

* A number of these are drawn from *The Dance of Intimacy*, a highly recommended book by Harriet Goldhar Lerner (1989).

"I yam what I yam." —Popeye

One of the most emotionally damaging experiences a person can encounter is *invalidation*. Many of us have been told (in one way or another) "You *shouldn't* be so emotional," "You *should* stop acting so childish," "You *should* be ashamed of yourself," "Who the hell do you think you are?!"

You are who you are. Yet all of us are sometimes greeted with such statements of criticism, shame, and invalidation. The message that comes through is, "Who you are (how you act or feel) is not okay. You should be *ashamed*." These reactions from others can have a powerful impact on the self, especially in childhood. In the wake of a shaming and critical comment, many young people turn inward, grit their teeth, ignore inner feelings and comply. The *true self* is stifled, and may remain underdeveloped.

Conversely, acceptance, validation, and affirmation from others act powerfully to relieve suffering. To feel accepted, to feel believed, to have others understand—all these provide tremendous emotional support at times of despair, helping us to recognize and develop our own "true selves."

One of the reasons therapy can be of such value is that good therapists provide acceptance, belief, and understanding—validation of who you are. Validation, however, comes not only from others, but also from within yourself. A crucial aspect of strengthening your "self" is to *allow yourself to believe your inner experiences.* Many people may think, "I shouldn't feel this way," or "I'm making mountains out of mole hills," when the simple truth is that they hurt. Self-validation is *acknowledging* your inner feelings and *accepting* them as real and understandable. It certainly does not mean that in any way you *like* the experience, that you choose to wallow in the pain, or that you accept the pain as your "lot in life." It is merely an open and honest acknowledgment of your emotional reality. Awareness and acknowledgment of inner truths can serve as an anchor during hard times. "I yam what I yam."

Speak Up!

A second step to take in strengthening your sense of self is to find outlets for *honest self-expression*. Weak muscles can gradually become strengthened by exercising. Self-expression is the type of emotional exercise that gradually builds and strengthens the self. Another major benefit of psychotherapy comes from your ability to clarify your inner feelings, needs, and beliefs and to voice these out loud with your therapist. This single experience can leave you feeling more real and solid about yourself.

Honest self-expression also means open verbal communication with others in your life; assertively expressing your opinions, beliefs, values, needs, taking a stand, saying "no," asking for change in others' behavior (see chapter 13).

Keep Track

Many people have found tremendous value in keeping a *personal journal*. Writing down feelings, thoughts, hopes, and dreams can be a powerful way to clarify inner emotional experiences and find an outlet for self-expression.

Take Care of Yourself

The self flourishes best in a healthy atmosphere, which you can create by giving yourself permission to *care for basic physical and emotional needs*: adequate rest, good nutrition, exercise, fresh air, surrounding yourself with things of beauty; making a place in your home that can be a haven of warmth, comfort, and peace; making time for recreation, humor, or relaxation; establishing a reasonable balance between work and play; setting realistic expectations for yourself; and, from time to time, splurging. All of these sound incredibly simple and obvious, but these issues often go unnoticed (even by psychologists who write self-help books) and can contribute to an underlying sense of dis-ease. Some people may think these ideas sound selfish. If so, it's a smart kind of selfishness since it helps people feel better, more alive, and in the long run, affects the lives of others in a positive way, too.

Get Involved

Finally, and as important as any of the ideas in this chapter, you may strengthen your sense of self by *becoming involved in life activities* that express and affirm your own inner beliefs and values. You may accomplish this through your choice of career. Many people realize this goal through involvement in churches, organizations, and causes that have personal meaning. Dozens of volunteer agencies and support programs in every community offer hundreds of opportunities for each of us to give something back to the world. Not only can these activities help the community, but they also can become an important vehicle for your own self-expression. Making a positive contribution to others, connecting with the world beyond yourself, is arguably the best way to begin to feel better about yourself.

Your journey through difficult times—with or without therapy—is easier when you feel a more solid sense of yourself.

Part IV

Are Medications
The Answer?

Chapter 18

A Brief Guide to Psychiatric Medications

T HESE DAYS YOU don't have to be seriously mentally ill to be prescribed psychiatric medications. In mental health clinics across the country, millions of people are being helped by brief therapy and benefiting from the appropriate use of certain psychiatric mediations. Let's see what this is all about.

Research, especially during the past decade, has made it clear that the symptoms of *some* major mental disorders are related to chemical changes in the brain. Examples: psychotic disorders, panic disorder, depression, manic depressive (bipolar) illness, attention deficit disorder. As millions of people can attest, gritting your teeth, trying harder, or using willpower simply doesn't work to overcome these painful symptoms.

Renowned psychiatrist Dr. Roy Menninger is credited with the observation that medications will probably never be developed that can fill empty lives or mend broken hearts. There is no kind of medication that can give a person a sense of connection with other human beings, a feeling of self, or the kind of values that make life worth living. At the same time, many newly developed psychotropic medications can dramatically affect the course of a person's life in a positive sense, and can help some people achieve better outcomes in brief therapy.

Be an Informed Consumer

Many people do not need medication; on the other hand, many folks are helped tremendously with this type of treatment. We want you to be well informed about the role of medication in brief therapy so you can make decisions about the possible use of psychiatric medications in your own treatment (for a comprehensive guide to psychiatric medication treatment see *Consumer's Guide to Psychiatric Drugs* by Preston, O'Neal, and Talaga, New Harbinger Publications, 2000).

In the past, patients were given prescriptions by the doctor and simply told, "Take these and call me if you don't get better." These days, everyone is more sophisticated. Today's patients want and need to know what to expect from medication treatment, the risks and benefits, and the possible side effects. In our view, this a healthy development. Rather than being a "passive patient," it makes more sense to be actively involved in your treatment, to be knowledgeable, to ask questions, and to collaborate with your doctor as you work together to solve problems. In this chapter, we'll give you the basics about psychiatric medications, so you can ask your doctor good questions about any and all concerns you may have about pursuing this aspect of treatment. When used appropriately, psychiatric medications make an enormous difference in reducing some types of human misery.

Psychiatric medications don't treat all forms of emotional pain. We'll focus here on those particular disorders that respond well to drug treatment, beginning with anxiety and depression, the most commonly encountered emotional problems.

Depression

Many people suffer from mild bouts of depression that may last a few days to a few weeks. However more serious forms of depression can last for months or years unless properly treated. Three types of depression have been shown to respond well to antidepressant medication treatment.

Major Depression

Moderate to severe depression that may last for many months if not treated. Antidepressant medications can be effective in more than 80 percent of cases of major depression. This is especially true if any of the following symptoms are present (these are symptoms that therapists look for to determine if medication treatment is warranted):

- Extreme sadness, despair, or irritability
- Unusual sleep habits: severe insomnia or excessive sleeping
- Pronounced fatigue
- Appetite changes (with either weight gain or weight loss)
- Loss of sex drive
- An inability to experience joy or pleasure
- Strong suicidal ideas

Dysthymia

This long-term, low-grade depression often begins in adolescence and may last a lifetime. Studies have shown that about 55 percent of people who suffer from dysthymia have a good response to antidepressants. The symptoms include:

- Negative, pessimistic thinking
- Low self-esteem; feelings of inadequacy
- Low energy and fatigue
- Lack of motivation and enthusiasm
- A decreased zest for life

Bipolar (Manic-Depressive) Disorder

This is a very serious psychiatric condition that causes extreme mood swings, from severe depression to episodes of mania (extra-high energy, agitation, decreased need for sleep, rapid speech, racing thoughts). All people with suspected bipolar disorder *must* be evaluated by a psychiatrist, and the disorder *must be treated with medications* (generally antidepressants and a mood stabilizer such as lithium or Depakote). Without medical treatment, people with bipolar disorder typically become progressively worse, and this grave disorder, if not treated, has a very high suicide rate.

Antidepressant Medications

Many forms of depression involve a biochemical malfunction in the brain. Antidepressants are a class of medication that have been shown to be highly effective in restoring normal brain functioning and reducing a number of depressive symptoms. It is important to note the following:

- Antidepressants are *not* tranquilizers. *Unless anxiety is a major component, tranquilizers are not an appropriate treatment for depression.*

- Antidepressants are *not* addictive.

- When prescribed they *must* be taken every day (as prescribed) if they are to work.

- When taking antidepressants patients are advised not to drink alcoholic beverages, since alcohol interferes with the effectiveness of the drug.

- Antidepressants (unfortunately) do not work overnight. It typically takes two to four weeks to notice the first signs of improvement. It's essential to know this so you won't feel discouraged during the first couple of weeks.

- If one antidepressant medication does not work, there are many other options. Most people can be successfully

Antidepressant Medications

Generic	Brand
imipramine	Tofranil
desipramine	Norpramin
amitriptyline	Elavil
nortriptyline	Aventyl
nortriptyline	Pamelor
protriptyline	Vivactil
trimipramine	Surmontil
doxepin	Sinequan
doxepin	Adapin
maprotiline	Ludiomil
amoxapine	Asendin
trazodone	Deseyrel
fluoxetine	Prozac
bupropion	Wellbutrin
sertraline	Zoloft
paroxetine	Paxil
venlafaxine	Effexor
nefazodone	Serzone
mirtazapine	Remeron
citalopram	Celexa
reboxetine	Vestra

MAO Inhibitors

phenelzine	Nardil
tranylcypromine	Parnate

treated, although sometimes two to three medications must be tried in order to find the right drug for the patient's unique biochemical and emotional needs.

- Once symptoms have significantly improved, it is important to continue taking the medication for at least six months to avoid relapse.

- Antidepressants are not "happy pills." They simply operate to restore normal biological functioning (improved sleep, appetite, and energy levels).

- Antidepressants restore normal functioning in the brain (much like insulin helps diabetics function normally). This treatment should not be seen as a "chemical crutch," but rather a medical treatment that effectively returns one to normal biological functioning.

- Side effects of antidepressants are generally mild and not dangerous and will vary depending on what medication is used, but may include drowsiness, dry mouth, and mild nausea. Ask your physician/psychiatrist for a list of specific side effects that may occur with the particular medication prescribed for you.

Anxiety and Panic

Not all types of anxiety are effectively treated by medication; however, two types of anxiety disorders have been shown to respond well:

Panic Disorder: This disorder is characterized by brief episodes of intense panic that come on suddenly and usually last for only a few minutes (typically 5-20 minutes). During an attack, a person may experience the following symptoms:

- Trembling, nervousness, panic

- Shortness of breath and a smothering sensation

- Rapid heartbeat, lightheadedness, dizziness

- A fear of impending doom (often the belief that "I'm going to die" or "I'm going crazy")

Panic is a terribly unpleasant disorder that, thankfully, is very treatable with certain psychiatric medications.

Anti-Panic Medications: Psychotropic drugs used to treat panic include two options:

- *Antidepressants* (see chart, page 143): All antidepressants have been shown to effectively treat panic disorder with one exception, the drug bupropion. All of the statements made earlier regarding antidepressant treatment also apply to the treatment of panic attacks. It must be emphasized that antidepressants must be taken on a daily basis and it generally requires 2-4 weeks of treatment before panic symptoms begin to diminish.

- *High-Potency Tranquilizers:* The tranquilizers alprazolam (Xanax) and clonazepam (Klonopin) are fast-acting medications that are quite effective in treating panic disorder. Often panic attacks can be reduced or eliminated within a few days of starting treatment with these medications. However, tranquilizers have three major problems. The first is drowsiness. The second is that they should never be discontinued abruptly. Finally, tranquilizers can be addictive. However, this typically only occurs in people who have a history of prior drug or alcohol abuse (or people who have a lot of biological relatives with drug and alcohol abuse problems). Generally in these cases, tranquilizers should not be used.

It makes sense to actively be involved in your treatment, to be knowledgeable, to ask questions, and to collaborate with your doctor as you work together to solve problems.

Psychiatrists often find a combination of antidepressant and tranquilizer quite successful.

The majority of people suffering from panic disorder must take medications for at least one year and often longer.

Severe Anxiety Following Major Life Crises: Short-term use of tranquilizers (in addition to brief therapy) is sometimes recommended in the wake of serious life crises. The medications are used (often for only a couple of weeks) to target two main symptoms: insomnia (especially difficulty falling asleep), and *nervousness* and *restlessness*. A list of commonly used tranquilizers follows:

Anxiety Medications

Generic	Brand
For nervousness	
buspirone	BuSpar
chlordiazepoxide	Librium
oxazepam	Serax
clorazepate	Tranxene
lorazepam	Ativan
prazepam	Centrax
alprazolam	Xanax
clonazepam	Klonopin
For insomnia	
flurazepam	Dalmane
temazepam	Restoril
triazolam	Halcion
quazepam	Doral
zolpidem	Ambien
estazolam	Prosom
zaleplon	Sonata

- As with antidepressants, patients should not drink alcohol when taking these medications.

- These should not be used in individuals with a drug or alcohol abuse history (except the drug buspirone).

- Never discontinue treatment abruptly. Always check with your physician before stopping treatment.

Other Disorders

We've focused primarily on the treatment of anxiety and depression in this chapter. Other emotional and psychiatric disorders can be successfully treated with psychiatric medications, however *typically not within the context of brief therapy*. In this section we will briefly list the symptoms of several disorders and medication options. Please refer to the books noted in the References section for details on drug treatment for various psychiatric disorders.

Obsessive-Compulsive Disorder

Recurring, persistent unpleasant or senseless thoughts or impulses that are difficult to prevent or ignore. Behaviors include repetitive actions or rituals carried out in an attempt to reduce obsessive ideas (repeatedly checking to see if doors and windows are locked; repeatedly washing hands).

Medication Options

Generic	Brand
clomipramine	Anafranil
fluoxetine	Prozac
sertraline	Zoloft
paroxetine	Paxil
fluvoxamine	Luvox
citalopram	Celexa

Bulimia

Binge eating followed by: self-induced vomiting, laxative use, strict dieting, or excessive exercise to prevent weight gain.
Medication Options: Antidepressants

Psychotic Disorders

(including schizophrenia, some forms of bipolar disorder and paranoia). These serious forms of mental illness have such symptoms as:

- Hallucinations, bizarre or unrealistic thoughts
- Confusion and grossly impaired judgment
- Agitation or chaotic behavior

Medication Options: Antipsychotic medications, such as chlorpromazine (Thorazine), haloperidol (Haldol), risperidone (Risperdal), quetiapine (Seroquel), clozapine (Clozaril), or olanzapine (Zyprexa).

Post-Traumatic Stress Disorder (PTSD)

This disorder often includes a rather characteristic group of symptoms in response to exposure to life events that were either extremely dangerous or frightening and/or in which a person encountered a tremendous sense of powerlessness. The event may be a recent trauma or may be an event that occurred many years earlier. [In the latter case, a person may massively block out the memory and feelings of the original event(s), which begin to surface months or years later in the form of intrusive memories or dreams.]
Symptoms of PTSD include:

- Vivid re-experiencing of the traumatic event in thoughts, recollections, or nightmares
- Avoiding situations that remind one of the traumatic event

- Memory impairment (amnesia of the event)
- Feelings of numbness, detachment, and unreality
- Intense feelings of anxiety, irritability, or depression
  Medication Options: Antidepressants; some tranquilizers

You're Calling the Shots

As an informed consumer and collaborator in your own medication treatment, remember—you're calling the shots. It's *your choice* whether or not to take psychotropic medication. *You* know how you respond to the treatment (positive effects and, at times, side effects). Discuss freely with your therapist any concerns you have about this part of treatment.

PART V

Managing Under Managed Care

Chapter 19

Finding Your Way through the Managed Care Maze

Brief THERAPY HAS been around for many years, in one form or another. Why is it suddenly so popular? The answers are simple, and incredibly complex, *time* and *money*.

Everyone feels the press of time these days. We all want to deal with problems quickly and get on with our lives. Brief therapy can't solve all the problems we face but, as you've seen in this book, it can be a great help. This makes brief therapy a very attractive option.

"Brief" is also generally seen as "cost-effective." With health care costs escalating out of sight, procedures that provide effective treatment at low cost are in great demand. Private and government health insurance programs and health care organizations have looked for every possible way to cut costs, and "cost-effective" has become a mantra repeated by regulators, health professionals, and patients alike.

The system that evolved in response to these demands has come to be known as "managed care." For better or for worse, the "managers" are the outfits that pay the bills—your employer who chooses medical care policies, insurance companies, government agencies, health maintenance organizations.

With the advent of managed care, health care as many of us have known it is forever changed. The "good old days" of the sixties, seventies, eighties—when you could see any physician or health care provider and have your insurance pick up the tab—are long gone for most of us.

And you're not exempt from some of these changes if you use a public hospital or university counseling center, or even if you pay for your own health care. The new system has changed more than just the way the bills are paid. The pace of everything is faster now, and all benefits are subject to careful evaluation and review. Doctors don't have much time to "visit" with patients anymore. Health care, including psychotherapy, follows a briefer problem-solving model more than ever before.

In the mental health field, new brief care standards have become routine in independent and group private practice, community mental health centers, college and university counseling centers and health clinics, public and private hospital psychiatry departments . . . virtually anywhere mental health professionals practice.

For simplicity in this chapter, we'll discuss all brief therapy settings as "managed care," although university centers and other public agencies may not use that term. There will, of course, be differences among various agencies, but the process of intake, referral, planning, and evaluation—and the headaches of paperwork—are similar.

Keep in mind that the discussion in this chapter refers to programs of therapy that are covered as benefits under a health care plan. You can get virtually any therapy you want or need if you are able and willing to pay for it yourself.

What Mental Health Benefits Are Available under Managed Care?

Most managed care companies and agencies offer restricted mental health benefits. You can't just pick up a phone book and choose a doctor or counselor. And you can't get coverage for all conditions. Getting what you need under managed care is rarely as simple as the ads for your care plan would have you believe!

To ensure you have as much information as possible and can make educated choices as a proactive, responsible partner in obtaining your own care, read your benefits book *carefully* and *completely*, until you understand it. Ask questions. Don't be afraid to advocate for what you want; to ask questions about your benefits, services that seem to be missing, how to obtain *any* particular benefit. Most managed care organizations are willing to spend time with you on the phone to help you understand what services you are eligible for and how to access them.

Typical mental health conditions covered under managed care tend to be those that require an *immediate* intervention:

- *Emergency care*—for patients who may be dangerous to themselves or others
- *Acute care*—for short-term life crises
- *Marital or family conflict*—especially if abuse is involved
- *Brief solution-focused problem solving*
- *Assessment and referral for chronic mental illness*—screening for long-term therapy

How Can You Make Managed Care Work for You?

For you, as a consumer and client, the easiest, most useful way to get services is to educate yourself regarding several basic aspects and limitations of the managed care model.

When you want or need to seek emotional support under your health care plan, remember that there is almost always a "protocol" to follow: a specific set of predictable steps and tasks you *must* follow in order to get services.

Often the mental health benefit (or "behavioral health" benefit as it is often called) requires a referral from your "primary care" physician. Thus, under the managed care plan, you can no longer simply see *any* licensed mental health professional, but must first request this service from your insurance plan, directly or through your primary care physician. The primary care provider is often (but not always) a general or family practitioner who has been assigned primary responsibility for your health care. In most plans, any referral to a needed specialist, including a psychotherapist, must come from your primary care provider. (In *some* plans, Kaiser, student counseling centers, a referral from a physician is not required.)

The thinking behind this "gatekeeper" approach is that by paying a general or family practitioner to handle most aspects of your care, the funding agency has a better handle on your actual medical needs.*

Help At Last!

When you get your referral it will often be directly to a Department of Psychiatry (if you belong to a "staff"-based

---

*   Often these physicians are entitled to provide care to a group of employees at a set monthly amount per person (or per capita, hence the trade term, "capitated care"). The fee does not fluctuate based upon the number of patients who come into the office or need the service of specialists.

model like Kaiser-Permanente), or to a specific group (if you belong to a "panel"-based model like Champus—a "panel" is a list of independent providers and practice groups who are approved by the plan). Most referrals are for a limited number of sessions, encouraging psychotherapists who work in managed care to adopt a brief therapy model.

Your therapist's first job, regardless of the model used as the basis of providing treatment, is to understand and assess as quickly as possible what is troubling you and how best to treat you. Based upon the initial assessment, the therapist will develop a "treatment plan" designed to assist you. In managed care, the treatment plan is based on resolving your current condition within the limits of your health benefits plan. After the number of therapy sessions called for in the treatment plan, additional sessions must be authorized through the managed care system's review process, and will be allowed *only* if need is shown. The assumption is that some difficulties can be addressed adequately in as few as one to three sessions. Managed care incorporates a system of checks and balances designed to ensure continuing access to care only if the company agrees with your therapist that such care is necessary *and* fits within the scope of your benefit plan.

Two basic ingredients typical of most managed care models are designed to insure that you are getting the best necessary treatment within the limitations of the plan: *utilization review* and *case management*. Both of these mechanisms require your therapist (aka "provider") to get permission or "preauthorization" from a representative of the health plan before providing certain diagnostic or therapeutic intervention. The intent is not to delay care, but to monitor the cost, necessity, and quality of your care. Unfortunately, this also means more paperwork and telephone time for your therapist outside of your sessions.

. . . You may have to be an active partner in the pursuit of the assistance you need . . . It can be empowering to accept responsibility as an active participant in your own care.

Privacy and confidentiality—traditional cornerstones of the therapeutic relationship—are a bit shaky in the new managed care environment. (There are also legal limits to confidentiality. See Appendix A for a typical therapist's confidentiality statement.) If you elect to have your health care plan pay for your brief (or other) psychotherapy, the plan's representative may become, in effect, a "third party" in the therapist's office. In other words, confidentiality in the traditional sense, your right to privacy, may be compromised if your insurance company is to pay. These days, insurance companies and other payors often require fairly detailed information about therapy clients and their treatment in order to determine whether or not to authorize additional sessions. This is in response to the need to monitor costs, yet it also is a practice many therapists *strongly* oppose. Please feel free to talk to your therapist about this issue so you can be assured regarding the degree of confidentiality.

Whether you're trying to get a first appointment authorized or your therapist has requested additional visits, you may have to be an active partner in the pursuit of the assistance you need by talking directly with your health plan's representative.

While the red tape can be frustrating, it can be empowering to accept responsibility as an active participant in your own care. Just as your brief treatment will be focused and quite specific, so will the steps required of you to obtain treatment on your behalf within a managed care benefit. Taking the time to understand these steps as a knowledgeable and educated consumer *before* you actually need help or assistance will maximize the possibility of a relatively straightforward, uncomplicated process at a time of need—when a minimum of stress may be crucial.

How Can You Tell If You're Getting Good Care?

There are some standards that may be applied to any health care situation to help you determine if you're getting quality care. Most managed care agencies use some or all of the following criteria to balance the "cost-effectiveness" equation:

- Informed consent of the patient, with ample information provided at the outset
- Assurance of confidentiality (see Appendix A)
- Careful assessment and treatment planning.
- Objective evaluation procedures (tests, surveys, peer review by other professionals)
- Research support for treatment procedures (literature references should be available if you ask)

Putting It All Together

Now let's take a look at a few examples of folks accessing their managed mental health benefits:

George is a twenty-seven-year-old whose wife has just left him. He had never been married before, nor seen or even considered seeing a counselor. He comes from a fairly conservative background and thought only "crazy" people see shrinks, but has never been this upset before either. He is having a hard time at work, his mind wanders, he is having difficulty sleeping and always feels tired. He doesn't know whom to talk with or even if he wants to talk. He decides that if only he could get some rest things would be better so he decides to see his doctor. His physician examines him and refers him to a counselor; he feels even more upset, as he had just wanted something to help him sleep. As he leaves the office, the nurse asks him what kind of insurance he has. He gives her his insurance card and she hands him a referral slip (or "preauthorization") for three visits. His insurance works with a "preferred provider panel" so he can look in his "participating provider book" and contact any conveniently located counselor listed. She reminds him that it is important when calling to tell the counselor not only the doctor who referred him, but the kind of insurance he has. He thinks about it, has another difficult evening, reluctantly calls the next day, and gets an appointment for later in the week. By the second visit he vows he made the right decision. While he is still struggling, he has found talking helpful. The homework his therapist assigned has been useful and he feels better doing something to take charge of his life. Toward the end of the visit, both George and the therapist decide that it would be helpful if their work could continue so the therapist requests preauthorization for several additional visits, reminding him to work hard between sessions, as time is short and "every session counts."

Alicia is a nineteen-year-old sophomore at a state university. An average student, her attention has recently been focused on her boyfriend, Alan. She arrived at the university psychological clinic after a referral by her dorm counselor when she began talking about suicide. Alan left school, joined the Army, and told Alicia to "start dating other guys." She was devastated, and says her life is over. The sensitive receptionist at the clinic connected Alicia immediately with the "intake counselor," who did an initial assessment of her condition and the likelihood that she would carry through on her threat. The counselor spent nearly two hours with Alicia, then walked her to the campus physician's office for a physical evaluation and possible anti-depressant medication. Alicia signed a short "contract" with the counselor, promising that she would not make any attempts on her life at least until she visited the counselor again in two days. The counselor consulted with the director of the clinic and with the referral physician. They developed a preliminary treatment plan for Alicia, involving three more sessions, another visit with the physician, a follow-up with the dorm counselor, and a short battery of psychological tests. After this short-term plan, Alicia *will be re-evaluated to determine her need for continuing therapy at the clinic or in an outside treatment center. (This state university's counseling policy allows only eight visits before referral to an outside agency.)*

Chuck *is eleven years old and has always been a good kid but has been having a hard time recently. For the last several years he has had increasing difficulty staying still in class or paying attention. He has become more impulsive and impatient at home. His parents, with the teacher's support, take him to see his pediatrician at Kaiser. After hearing the history, the doctor refers them to the Department of Psychiatry for an evaluation. They see Dr. Smith, a child psychologist, who has Chuck's parents and teacher fill out a long questionnaire. Dr. Smith reviews the records and family history, interviews the family and Chuck, and administers several psychological tests. She then refers Chuck to a child psychiatrist for a medication consultation. The decision is made to see if Chuck would benefit from a trial on medication, and the family continues to talk with Dr. Smith, who assigns a number of "homework assignments" to the family in their weekly meetings. Six weeks later Chuck's parents and teacher report that he is doing much better. Dr. Smith refers Chuck to his pediatrician, rescheduling the family for a routine follow-up appointment in three months.*

Taking Charge of Your Own Care

Basically, that's it. If you remember that *every session counts* and work hard to make the most of every one, many difficulties can improve in a short time. Don't forget that every managed care plan will have its own unique way of doing things but, in general, to access your mental health benefits you will need to:

- See what kind of mental heath care your particular plan offers by reading the benefits book *entirely* and contacting your health care representative with any questions or concerns. This will verify your understanding as a consumer and patient. Find out if you need a physician referral to see a therapist.

- Make an appointment with your primary care physician and let him or her know you need emotional support and ask that rather than simply prescribing medication for you that he or she facilitate a referral to a mental health specialist.

- Set up an appointment with the department, group, or individual to which you have been referred.

- Work hard with your therapist, remembering that *every session counts*. Identify the problem(s) troubling you and work in collaboration with your therapist to determine the best course of action available to you. Follow through assertively!

- Remember both you and your therapist have responsibility for your care. Each of you needs to work actively at verifying compliance with the managed care plan guidelines if you want them to help pay for treatment.

Afterword

LIFE HOLDS THE promise of joy, the hope for meaningful relationships, and opportunities to contribute to others and the community at large. But life can also be very hard and sometimes tragic. Each person is doing her or his best to make it—to survive and to live the best life possible. Sometimes our attempts to cope are successful, but at other times the challenges are simply overwhelming. To be knocked over by life's stresses is no crime or sin, but it's no picnic either. No human being is immune to feeling overwhelmed.

Psychotherapy is a valuable resource for dealing with those stresses, and brief therapy has made it possible for more and more people to benefit from that resource. Brief therapy does not attempt to "cure" people, but it does facilitate effective coping and enhances our inherent capacities for emotional healing.

You've heard us say over and over that "every session counts." Let us close by saying "your life counts." When times are hard, you owe it to yourself to take constructive action that will help you make it. You may just find the most valuable action will be your decision to pursue brief therapy.

We hope this book has been helpful, and we wish you well.

—J.P., N.V., D.L.

Sample Therapist's Statement on Confidentiality

THE RIGHTS AND welfare of those who seek psychological services are protected by state law and the professional code of ethics to which I subscribe.

Essentially, this means that information about clients revealed in the course of psychotherapy or evaluation remains strictly confidential. That is, I will need a signed release prior to releasing information regarding you.

You should be aware, however, that the protection of confidentiality is not absolute. There are a few specific occasions, which arise quite rarely, when a therapist may be legally or ethically compelled to release information to another. For example, if it were the therapist's judgement that the client posed an imminent danger to himself or herself or to others, the therapist might need to notify the authorities, relatives, or an intended victim. In other instances a court would be entitled to client information if:

a) the court ordered and paid for the examination/evaluation, or

b) the client claimed in a legal action that his or her therapy was relevant to the outcome of that legal action.

Also, therapists may be required by law to report any suspected child abuse or sexual molestation to Child Protective Services or elder abuse to Adult Protection Services. Finally, the therapist cannot promise *absolute* confidentiality to a child or adolescent client supported by and living with his parents (unemancipated minor) in regard to matters of overriding importance to his or her welfare. For example, if a child was a danger to himself or herself or others, the therapist could not hold this information confidential.

In any case, it is highly unlikely that any of these unusual situations would arise. If they should, please be assured that I will discuss the matter with you and will seek your full participation in any decisions that may be required. I will exercise both sensitivity and professional judgment in releasing only the minimal amount of information required by the particular situation.

Self-Rating Checklist

ONE POTENTIALLY valuable and useful technique for accurately measuring how you are feeling is the use of "Self-Rating Checklist" like the one below. The items included are common difficulties many people experience, but not all will apply. Because we are each unique, you will find several "blanks" to fill in about uncomfortable areas you may want to focus on. This is a great technique to use at least once a week while in difficult times and will help you note changes and provide a realistic perspective on how you are doing at any point in time.

Self-Rating Checklist

Check only one answer to each question

0 = Not at all 1 = A little 2 = Somewhat 3 = Quite a bit 4 = A lot

During the past week, how much did you suffer from:

1. Difficulty catching your breath, or getting a lump in your throat   0 1 2 3 4

2. Chest pain, pressure, or feeling as though your heart may be racing   0 1 2 3 4

3. Excessive sweating for no reason, feeling lightheaded and/or dizzy   0 1 2 3 4

4. Feeling off balance or like your legs may not hold you up and you could fall   0 1 2 3 4

5. Nausea or stomach problems   0 1 2 3 4

6. Feeling detached or disconnected from yourself and/or others   0 1 2 3 4

7. Hot or cold flashes   0 1 2 3 4

8. Feeling as though you are dying or that something terrible could happen at any second   0 1 2 3 4

9. Believing you are or about to "lose it"   0 1 2 3 4

10. Worrying excessively about dirt, germs, or chemicals   0 1 2 3 4

11. Worrying that something bad will happen because you forgot something important like locking the door or turning something off   0 1 2 3 4

12. Unable to stop worrying that you will lose something that is really important to you   0 1 2 3 4

13. Excessive washing or wanting to wash yourself or things around you   0 1 2 3 4

14. Checking or wanting to check things over and over or repeat them to be sure   0 1 2 3 4

15. Avoiding or wanting to avoid situations or people   0 1 2 3 4

16. Finding yourself thinking about distressing things over and over again   0 1 2 3 4

17. Feeling isolated or alone   0 1 2 3 4

18. Feeling increasingly sad, blue, or depressed   0 1 2 3 4

19. Having little and/or no appetite or eating just because you know you should   0 1 2 3 4

20. Having difficulty enjoying things you normally do   0 1 2 3 4

21. Being increasingly forgetful and/or having difficulty concentrating   0 1 2 3 4

22. Sleeping more or less than you normally do and/or waking up tired   0 1 2 3 4

23. Thoughts of wanting to hurt yourself or wishing you were dead   0 1 2 3 4

24. Having upsetting recollections of a traumatic event   0 1 2 3 4

25. Having recurrent dreams of a traumatic event and/or feeling as though it might be happening again   0 1 2 3 4

26. Feeling irritable and easily frustrated   0 1 2 3 4

_____   0 1 2 3 4

_____   0 1 2 3 4

_____   0 1 2 3 4

_____   0 1 2 3 4

Group Programs
for Help with
Emotional Problems

In YOUR EFFORTS to deal with the emotional issues in your life, on your own and as a part of your brief therapy, you may find it helpful to consider participation in some form of group work. In most communities, there is a wide variety of therapy, self-help, and support groups available to assist with emotional problems. Such groups vary tremendously: some can be very helpful; others can *create* serious emotional problems for those seeking help.

For help in locating resources in your community, contact your local Mental Health Association. Check directory information or contact: The National Mental Health Association, 1021 Prince Street, Alexandria, VA 22314; phone (703) 684-7722.

Psychotherapy groups typically are led by a professional, licensed psychotherapist with specific training in group processes, psychotherapy, and group dynamics. Clients enter these groups on referral from a professional, usually as an integral part of ongoing therapy. Participation in a psychotherapy group may last from a few weeks to a year or more, depending upon the problem focus and the needs of the clients. Some groups are highly structured toward specific behavioral changes, others involve sharing of deep personal experiences and feelings; some deal with important current stressors, others with long-standing emotional and personality difficulties. With a good therapist, group treatment is powerful and can be very helpful.

Support groups abound. Many of these are either leaderless or are led by a non-professional and are often topical: bereavement, divorce, women's or men's issues. Such groups can provide considerable support and human connection for the members. Such groups should avoid in-depth exploration of emotional concerns; there is an inherent risk of psychiatric disaster should extremely intense issues emerge in a group with an untrained leader. Caution is advised. Self-help groups can be valuable, but if you think you *need professional* help, get it.

Organized self-help/recovery programs are often based on an established set of values, philosophies, and guidelines, such as the various twelve-step programs: Alcoholics Anonymous and its dozens of clones for gambling, obesity, "co-dependency," "sexual addiction" . . . Many professionals refer clients to these groups for specific needs. They can be very valuable, but here too, caution is advised.

Potential Benefits of Self-Help Group Program

- Validation of your feelings
- Emotional support
- Advice
- Guest speakers
- Networking
- Affordability

- Feedback
- Step-by-step strategies

Potential Risks of Self-Help Group Programs

- Intense emotional openness
- Re-creation of maladaptive patterns
- Charismatic or "cult" dependency
- "One-size-fits-all"
- No screening of members
- Unrealistic promises
- Religious/spiritual focus you don't agree with
- Avoidance of seeking professional treatment
- Long-term dependence on the group
- Promise of quick cures

Check out a group thoroughly before you join. Get references and recommendations just as you might in trying to locate a physician, dentist, or therapist. Talk to the group leader and a group member prior to your first meeting. And if you do decide to attend a group, consider the first meeting as a trial visit—check it out and see if it feels right for you. Ask questions!

References

Alberti, R., and M. Emmons. 1995. *Your Perfect Right*, 7th ed. San Luis Obispo, CA: Impact Publishers.

Beck, A.T. 1976. *Cognitive Therapy and the Emotional Disorders*. New York: New American Library.

Beck, A.T., and G. Emery. 1985. *Anxiety Disorders and Phobias: A Cognitive Perspective*. New York: Basic Books.

Benson, H. 1975. *The Relaxation Response*. New York: Avon.

Bower, S.A., and G.H. Bower. 1994. *Asserting Your Self*, 2nd ed. Reading, MA: Addison-Wesley Publishing Co.

Bradshaw, J. 1989. *The Family*. Deerfield Beach, FL: Health Communications.

Budman, S., and A. Gurman. 1988. *Theory and Practice of Brief Therapy*. New York: Guilford Publications.

Burns, D.D. 1980. *Feeling Good*. New York: Signet.

Davis, M., E.R. Eshelman, and M. McKay. 1995. *The Relaxation and Stress Reduction Workbook*, 4th ed. Oakland, CA: New Harbinger.

Frey, W.H., and C. Hoffman-Ahern. 1983. Crying behavior in the adult. *Integrative Psychiatry* 1:94–100.

Klerman, G.L., and M.M. Weissman. 1984. *Interpersonal Psychotherapy of Depression*. New York: Basic Books.

Lerner, H.G. 1989. *The Dance of Intimacy*. New York: Harper and Row.

Lewisohn, D.M. 1984. *The Coping with Depression Guide: A Psycho-educational Intervention for Unipolar Depression.* Eugene, OR: Castalia Press.

Peck, M.S. 1978. *The Road Less Traveled.* New York: Simon and Schuster.

Preston, J. 1993. *Growing Beyond Emotional Pain: Action Plans for Healing.* San Luis Obispo, CA: Impact Publishers.

Rakos, R.F., and H.E. Schroeder. 1980. *Self-Directed Assertiveness Training* audiotape. New York: Guilford Publications.

Shapiro, F. 1995. *Eye Movement Desensitization and Reprocessing: Basic Principles, Protocols, and Procedures.* New York: Guilford Press.

Strupp, H. 1969. Toward a specification of teaching and learning in psychotherapy. *Archives of General Psychiatry*, 21:203–212.

Wolpe, J., and D. Wolpe. 1988. *Life Without Fear.* Oakland, CA: New Harbinger Publications.

Regarding Medication Treatment

General Reference: Preston, J., J. O'Neal, and M. Talaga. 2000. *Consumer's Guide to Psychiatric Drugs.* Oakland, CA: New Harbinger Publications.

Depression: Preston, J. 1996. *You Can Beat Depression: A Guide to Recovery.* San Luis Obispo, CA: Impact Publishers.

Anxiety: Bourne, E. 1995. *The Anxiety & Phobia Workbook,* 2nd ed. Oakland, CA: New Harbigner.

Sheehan, D. 1983. *The Anxiety Disease.* New York: Bantam Books.

Bi-Polar: Fieve, R. 1989. *Moodswings.* New York: Bantam Books.

Psychosis: Mueser, K.T., and S. Gingerich. 1994. *Coping with Schizophrenia: A Guide for Families.* Oakland, CA: New Harbinger Publications.

Torrey, E.F. 1988. *Surviving Schizophrenia: A Family Manual.* New York: Harper and Row.

Obsessive-Compulsive Disorder: Rapoport, J. 1989. *The Boy Who Couldn't Stop Washing.* New York: Dutton.

Steketee, G., and K. White. 1990. *When Once Is Not Enough.* Oakland, CA: New Harbinger Publications.

John Preston, Psy.D., is a clinical psychologist and Dean of the Professional School of Psychology in Sacramento, California. He is the author of 10 books, including *You Can Beat Depression, Growing Beyond Emotional Pain,* and *Integrative Brief Therapy,* and is the co-author of *Handbook of Clinical Psychopharmacology for Therapists* and *Consumer's Guide to Psychiatric Drugs.* Dr. Preston is a former Chief Psychologist with the Kaiser Brief Therapy Clinic and has taught at the University of California at Davis School of Medicine.

Nicolette Varzos, Ph.D., has worked extensively as a researcher in the area of clinical psychology and has numerous publications in the field of mental health and rehabilitation. She is currently working in private practice in Sacramento, and specializes in neuropsychological and clinical assessment.

Douglas S. Liebert, Ph.D., is the Clinical Director of the Family Therapy Institute of Sacramento, Inc. In addition to an active clinical, supervision, and consultation practice, his academic appointments have included the Department of Psychiatry, School of Medicine, University of California, Davis; California State University, Sacramento; and the Professional School of Psychology.

More New Harbinger Titles

CONSUMER'S GUIDE TO PSYCHIATRIC DRUGS

This empowering guide explains how each drug works and tells you what to expect in terms of side-effects, interactions with other drugs, dietary restrictions, and danger signs.

Item CGPD Paperback, $16.95

THOUGHTS & FEELINGS

The second edition of this classic workbook covers all of the major cognitive-behavioral techniques for taking control of your moods and your life.

Item TF2 Paperback, $18.95

THE ANXIETY & PHOBIA WORKBOOK

This comprehensive guide is the book therapists most often recommend to clients struggling with anxiety disorders.

Item PHO2 $19.95

STOP WALKING ON EGGSHELLS

This guide for the family and friends of those who have borderline personality disorder helps them establish personal limits, cope with self-destructive behavior, and take care of themselves.

Item WOE Paperback $14.95

SURVIVOR GUILT

Helps survivors of traumatic events come to terms with feelings of guilt and cope with how they affect personal functioning and relationships.

Item SG Paperback, $14.95

Call **toll-free 1-800-748-6273** to order. Have your Visa or Mastercard number ready. Or send a check for the titles you want to New Harbinger Publications, 5674 Shattuck Avenue, Oakland, CA 94609. Include $3.80 for the first book and 75¢ for each additional book to cover shipping and handling. (California residents please include appropriate sales tax.) Allow four to six weeks for delivery.

PRICES SUBJECT TO CHANGE WITHOUT NOTICE.

Some Other New Harbinger Self-Help Titles